THE FINEST OF ALL

Local Men on the Somme
1st. July, 1916

Best Wishes
Fred Holcroft

Fred Holcroft

This edition published by:-

FRED HOLCROFT
Chickamauga
54, Pemberton Road,
Winstanley,
Wigan,
Lancashire
WN3 6DA
Tel:- (01942) 225077

© FRED HOLCROFT, 1995.

All rights reserved.
No part of the book may be reproduced or tramsmitted in any form without the written permission of the publisher

ISBN 0 9524311 2 2

Produced by;-
Ian Winstanley,
PICKS PUBLISHING,
83, Greenfields Crescent,
Ashton-in-Makerfield,
Wigan Lancashire.
WN4 8QY
Tel:- (01942) 723675

Printed by:-
Douglas Printers Ltd., Woodhouse Drive, Wigan, Lancashire.
Tel:- (01942) 246210

"No braver or more determined men ever faced an enemy than those who went over the top on the 1st. July, 1916. Never before had the ranks of the British Army on the field of battle contained the finest of all classes of the nation in physique, brains and education. All were volunteers."

British Official History of the War.

To
Peter Nolan,
for his encouragement.

CONTENTS

INTRODUCTION	1
CHAPTER I. The Somme.	2
CHAPTER II The Attack.	17
CHAPTER III Casualties.	28
CHAPTER IV Corps Attacks.	33
CHAPTER V The Fight Goes On.	66
CONCLUSIONS	80
THOSE WHO FELL, 1st. July, 1916.	84
IN EPITAPH	99
PHOTOGRAPHS	105

ACKNOWLEDGEMENTS

I would like to thank Frank Taylor who drew the maps and the front cover, Ian Winstanley who helped prepare the manuscript, John Gasson and Dennis Martland who helped to compile the Appendix and Dennis Martland who provided the transcript of the taped interview with the late Harry Holcroft.

Photographs.
Imperial War Museum, Photographs 3, 4, 5, 6.
Wigan Heritage Service, frontispiece and photographs, 1, 2, 7, 13, 14.
Michael Green, photographs, 15, 16.
Ken Bennett, photographs, 17, 19, 20.
Fred Holcroft, photographs, 8, 9, 10, 11, 12, 18.

WE: Wigan Examiner
WO: Wigan Observer
LC: Leigh Chronicle
LJ: Leigh Journal

MAPS

Map 1	The Western Front : 1915-1916.	3
Map 2	British Armies in France. : 1916	7
Map 3	The Somme Battlefield.	16
Map 4	Ground Gained : 1st. July, 1916.	27
Map 5	The Capture of Mantauban.	37
Map 6	XV Corps Attack.	44
Map 7	Beaumont Hamel.	54
Map 8	Ground Gained, July - November, 1916.	79

PHOTOGRAPHS

Writing home from the trenches.	Frontispiece
Volunteers drilling with wooden rifles.	9
Advancing in extended order.	13
German machine-gun crew.	19
Wounded soldiers from both sides return,	23
1/Lancashire Fusiliers on parade.	29
'Heaps of chalk'. German trenches.	35
Montauban. No-Man's-Land, 1916.	39
Montauban today.	40
Sunken road today. Seen from (3) on Map 7.	56
Beaumont Hamel today. Seen from (1) on Map 7.	58
Beaumont Hamel today. Seen from (2) on Map 7.	58
Hawthorne Crater today. Seen from (4) on Map 7.	60
Montauban. German trench just captured.	69
Montauban. Same trench now used by the British.	70
The author in a shell hole near Beaumont Hamel.	75
The author in former British trenches.	82
Thiepval Memorial.	85
Corporal Rowlands' grave in Leigh Cemetery.	93
Battlefield debris found at (5) on Map 7	97
Grave, Hawthorne Ridge, CWGC Cemetery.	104

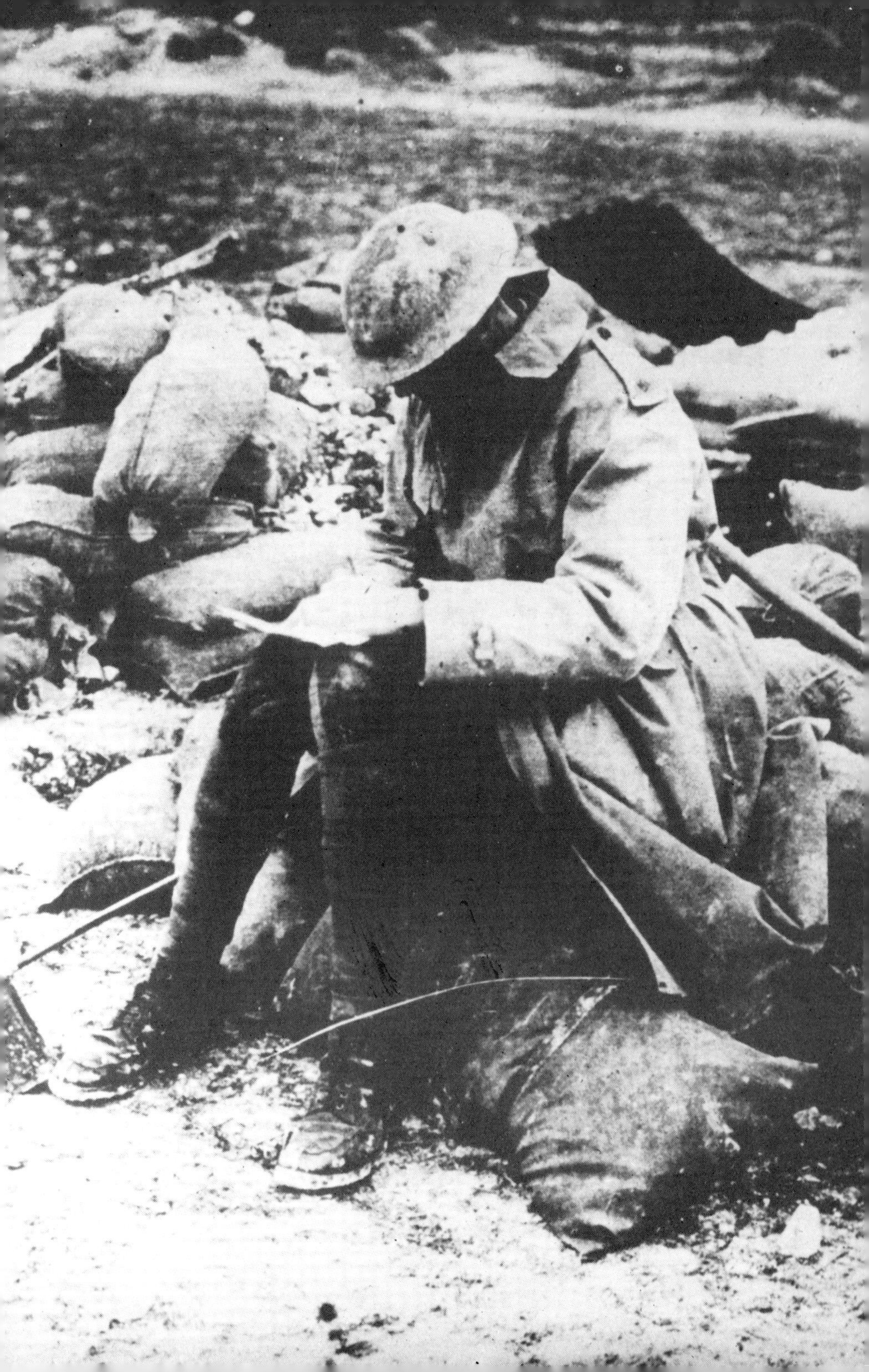

INTRODUCTION

The Battle of the Somme fought in 1916 occupies a special place in British military history. It was the first time since the Great War had begun in 1914 that British troops played a leading rather than a supporting role to the French in an offensive against the Germans on the Western Front and it was the first really significant battle fought by Great Britain's new mass army of volunteers drawn from every walk of life in the country by Kitchener's call to come forward. Because the causality lists were so huge, particularly on the opening day, the 1st. July, 1916 when almost 60,000 men were killed, wounded or missing, few campaigns have provoked so much controversy and emotive opinion. As the Somme battles dragged on, the losses on both sides mounted until eventually the scale of the fighting and the size of the casualties eclipsed even those of Verdun which has become a by-word for attrition.

	Somme	Verdun	Total
French	195,000	370,000	565,000
British	420,000		420,000
German	437,000	337,000	774,000
Total	1,052,000	707,000	1,759,000

By 1916 the British forces on the Western Front were the largest army that Great Britain had ever put into the field but because of the unforeseen scale of the fighting and the lack of peacetime preparation it was hastily trained and completely inexperienced in actual warfare. Most men had never held a rifle before in their lives.

Because such a large proportion of Great Britain's regular, territorial and volunteer divisions fought at one time or another in the Somme sector during the four and half months of the offensive, - over 50 divisions in all- most local men serving on the Western Front participated in the Battle of the Somme. As far as possible, this is an account of the fighting as seen through the eyes of those who were there, together with its impact on those left behind at home, told using the actual words of those local men who took part. This is their story.

Lest we forget.

CHAPTER I. The Somme.

In the summer of 1914 nothing seemed less likely to the British people than war. True there were pressing domestic problems; unemployment, strikes and industrial unrest, struggle for women's suffrage, turmoil in Ireland, but for a hundred years Great Britain had been at peace with her continental neighbours. Then in June, 1914, the assassination of Archduke Ferdinand of Austria in the Bosnian capital, Sarajevo, set in motion an incredible chain of events which plunged mainland Europe into war. When Germany violated Belgian neutrality Great Britain was drawn into the conflict. No one imagined that a four year war of attrition which would kill millions was about to commence. Great Britain sent an army to help France, superbly trained but by continental standards an incredibly small force (80,000), the 'contemptible little army' the Kaiser called it, arriving just in time to help push back the Germans from the outskirts of Paris. Both sides attempted to outflank the other, without success, and as the exhausted armies dug themselves into two continuous lines of trenches just a few hundred yards apart stretching from the Channel coast to the Swiss frontier, trench warfare was born.

Throughout the winter of 1914-15 the men struggled to adapt to this new type of fighting and a complicated mixture of news trickled back, some of it candid, some of it humorous, and some of it quite surreal. Private Walter Hardman from Wigan reported:-

> "It is very exciting (sic) when in the trenches. You hear shells flying over you in their hundreds and the bullets singing over your head or burying themselves in the trench wall in front of you. You have only to put your head up to finish this world's troubles."
> W.E. 2nd. Jan., 1915.

When the war began Horace Barker from Horwich was living in Paris and had volunteered for the French army. He graphically describes the hastily-dug trenches which only just stopped the German advance:-

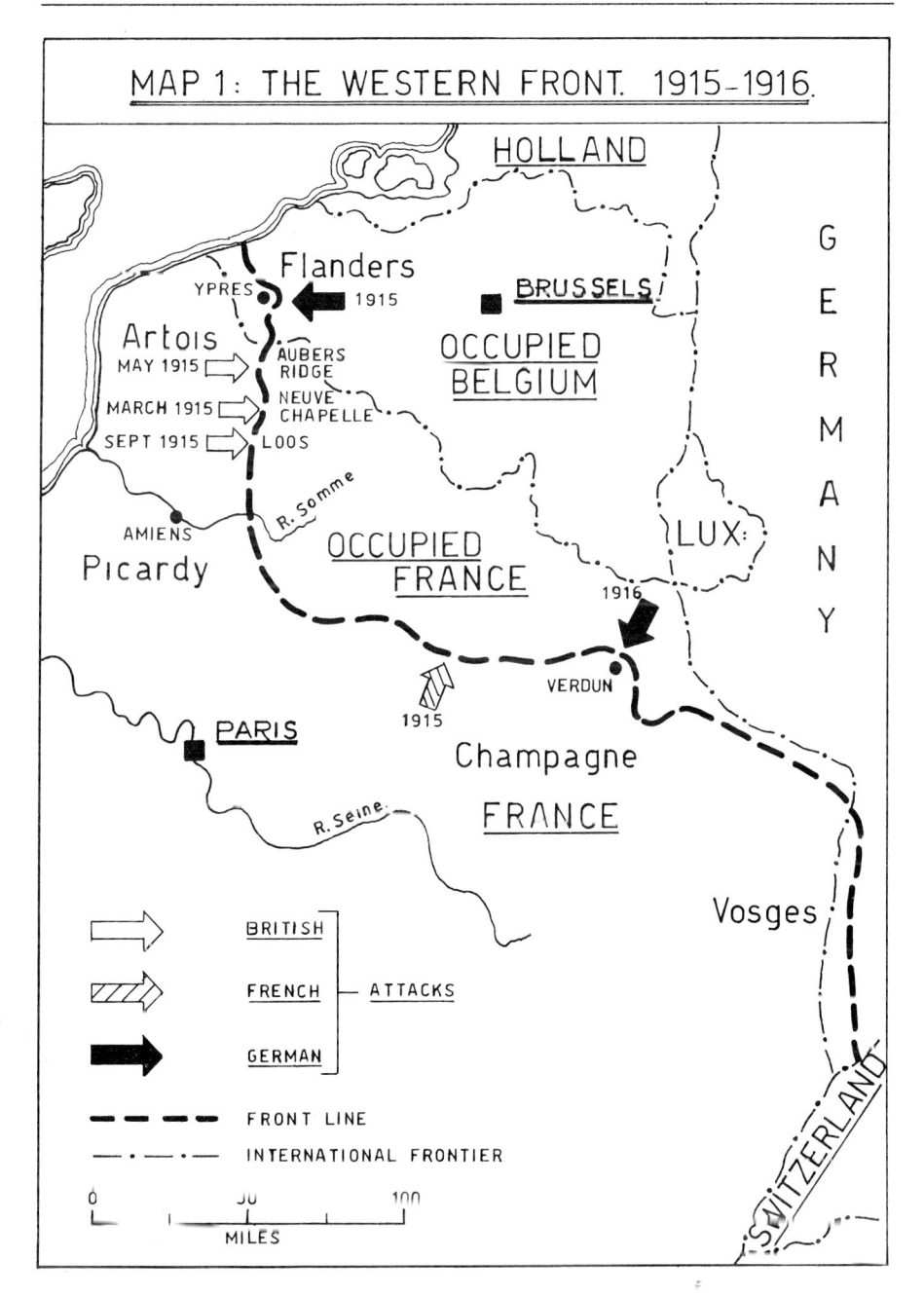

The Finest of All

MAP 1: THE WESTERN FRONT. 1915-1916.

> "They formed a square round the cemetery and were lined with coffins, the sides of the trenches had been cut through graves. The shells had also torn up some of the coffins and the sights were remarkable. The trenches were deep in mud and water and here and there a coffin stuck out."
> W.E. 26th. Jan., 1915.

Living conditions in the trenches were awful[1], with mud, water, poor sanitation and Private Mills from Leigh grew exasperated with the rather sanitised photographs appearing in the press:-

> "You will have seen pictures of the trenches in the illustrated papers. I don't know where they were taken but they give outsiders an erroneous view of things."
> L.J. 23rd. Apr., 1915.

The actual trench fighting was intense to the point of madness. Lance Corporal Rogers, a machine gunner in the 4th. Royal Irish Dragoon Guards, wrote home:-

> "After Thursday night's fighting I am lucky to be alive. We were told to blow up the German trench only 15 yards from us which we had mined. Our Maxim gun was in the forward trench and we had orders to open fire immediately the trench was blown up. Talk about an explosion! It lifted the ground from under us. It rained on our trench all sorts of things, mud, sods, and even German haversacks. The bodies of three Germans, legs and arms lying apart, were blown over the fir trees ten yards behind us. The noise was deafening. Our men took the trench that was blown up and captured the only three Germans left alive. The rest were blown to atoms."
> W.E. 13th. Mar., 1915.

Many more letters emphasise the dangers of trench warfare but by contrast others stressed the sheltered nature of life in the trenches. Several Hindley territorials, Thomas Worgan, Sam Edwards and Will

---

[1] Described more fully in the companion volume, 'They Lived With Death, Passchendaele'.

Marsden, all in the Loyal North Lancashires wrote home;-

> "You feel a bit timid going into the trenches for the first time but that soon passes and it's soon just like going to work."
> W.E. 3rd. Apr., 1915.

Private John Butterworth from Horwich in the same Regiment agreed:-

> "The trenches are as safe as houses. You can walk about in the daytime without fear of being hit as long as you are careful.'
> W.E. 6th. Apr., 1915.

This strange combination of unrelenting monotony and constant danger was broken on Christmas Day, 1914, in the most unusual affair of the entire war. Private Thomas Nash of the 1/East Lancashire Regiment described the incident to a reporter while recuperating from wounds in 'The Woodlands', a large house donated by Lord Crawford as a hospital:-

> "On Christmas Day we were in a place in Flanders having been in the same place for three months. About noon the Germans ceased firing and two or three of them came, unarmed, out of their trenches saying they wished to speak to us. Two or three of our chaps went to meet them. More unarmed Germans came across and our chaps then went out also unarmed to meet them, our officers warning them to take every precaution in case of treachery. A few men were left in our trenches with rifles in case of treachery but I was one of those who went out. There were four or five hundred Germans and about two hundred of us. We all shook hands and fraternised generally, exchanging Christmas greetings, cigarettes, cigars etc., several Germans exchanging watches for our jack-knives. Then our Commanding Officer came out and one of the German officers took a photograph of us all mixed up together, British and Germans. Our Commanding Officer arranged for a football match to take place on New Year's Day but I was relieved from the front line before then so I don't know if it took place or not. We were chatting to them for two hours and they told us that they were sorry that they were

fighting us but they fully expected to win. Some were London waiters and spoke very good English. We helped them to bury their dead."
W.O. 16th, January, 1915.

Harold Ainsworth of Hornby Street, Wigan received a letter from his nephew, a sapper in the front line, telling a similar story:-

"The Germans on our part of the line made a sort of truce. They had mot fired a shot up to last night (28th. December). They came halfway across No-Man's-Land and had a chat with our infantry on Christmas Eve, Boxing Day and exchanged cigarettes. We were out barb-wiring in front of our trench on Christmas Eve and Boxing Day and the two following nights, and although they must have seen us and surely heard us a mile away, they never fired a shot. They are very confident. They reckon they have already beaten the Russians."
W.O. 16th. January, 1915.

Corporal Prudence who lived near the Boar's Head, Standish got two cigars and a handkerchief as a present from two ex-waiters from Manchester!

In March, 1915 the British attacked at Neuve Chapelle and in April, 1915 the Germans counter attacked at Ypres. In May 1915 the British responded at Aubers Ridge and Festubert and again in September 1915 at Loos while simultaneously the French made their only attack of 1915 in Champagne. In two incredible years losses[1] rocketed:-

	British	French	German
1914	86,000	850,000	650,000
1915	300,00	1,000,000	700,000

All attacks failed hopelessly, despite meticulous planning. Defence dominated the battlefield. A combination of barbed-wire, artillery and machine-guns defeated all offensive efforts and both sides settled

[1] Killed, wounded, missing.

The Finest of All

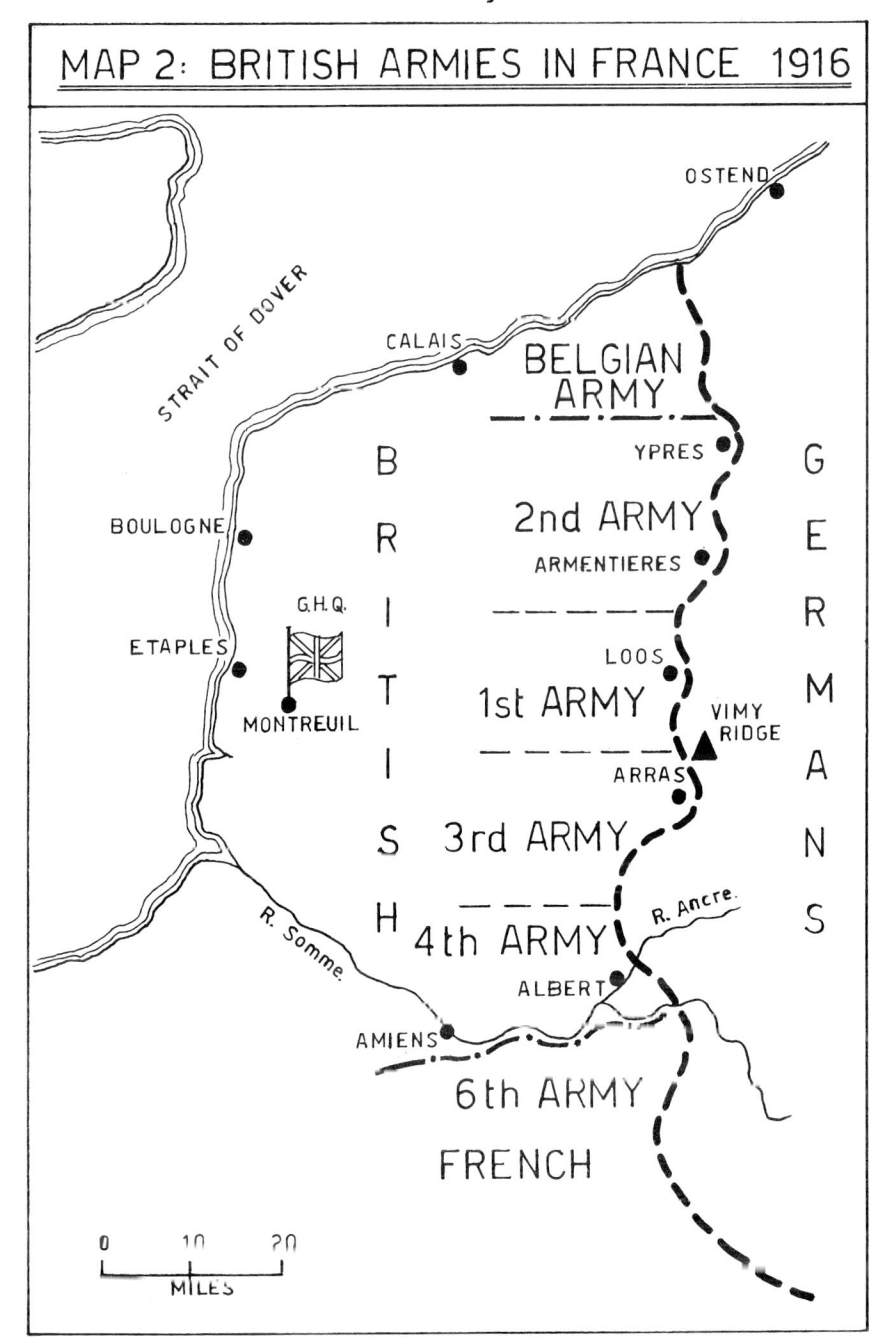

MAP 2: BRITISH ARMIES IN FRANCE 1916

down to a second winter of trench warfare while their generals planned for 1916.

The Allies had just agreed to a French plan for simultaneous offensives on all fronts when the Germans struck first. In February 1916, they attacked Verdun and although their initial assault failed, the Germans persisted in an attempt to wear the French down. On other fronts too, in Russia, Italy and Serbia, the Allies were pushed back and only British troops were available for an offensive. The valley of the River Somme, a sector of the front inactive since 1914, was chosen as the place to make not merely a diversion but a decisive breakthrough, the 'Big Push.'

Once the front and general nature of the attack had been fixed and military preparations fully completed, only one question remained. The attack was to be made by General Rawlinson's Fourth Army of whose fifteen divisions only two were of regular soldiers. Two more divisions were territorials intended for home defence who had agreed to serve overseas and although they had trained part-time in civilian life whilst holding down a regular job, except for a few former soldiers, none of the territorials had experienced actual fighting. A further ten divisions, two thirds of the army, consisted of thousands of former civilians who had rushed to respond to Kitchener's appeal for volunteers back in August, 1914. Also taking part were two territorial divisions belonging to General Allenby's Third Army which were to protect the northern (left) flank. Although the total strength of the British Army on the Continent was now a million men, 16 of the 38 divisions had only experienced trench warfare and had yet to go 'over the top' in an attack.

Local men had swamped the Wigan recruiting office, the premises of George Healy and Sons, Auctioneers at the corner of Grimes' Arcade and Bretherton Row, with as much enthusiasm as anywhere in the country. Within a fortnight over a thousand men had volunteered, within a month two thousand had signed up at the rate of fifty a day, mainly coal miners, not just from Wigan but from all over the district. By mid-November the total had reached 4,700. Then suddenly the flow dried up and despite all appeals from local dignitaries only a trickle came in before Christmas. In the New Year another determined

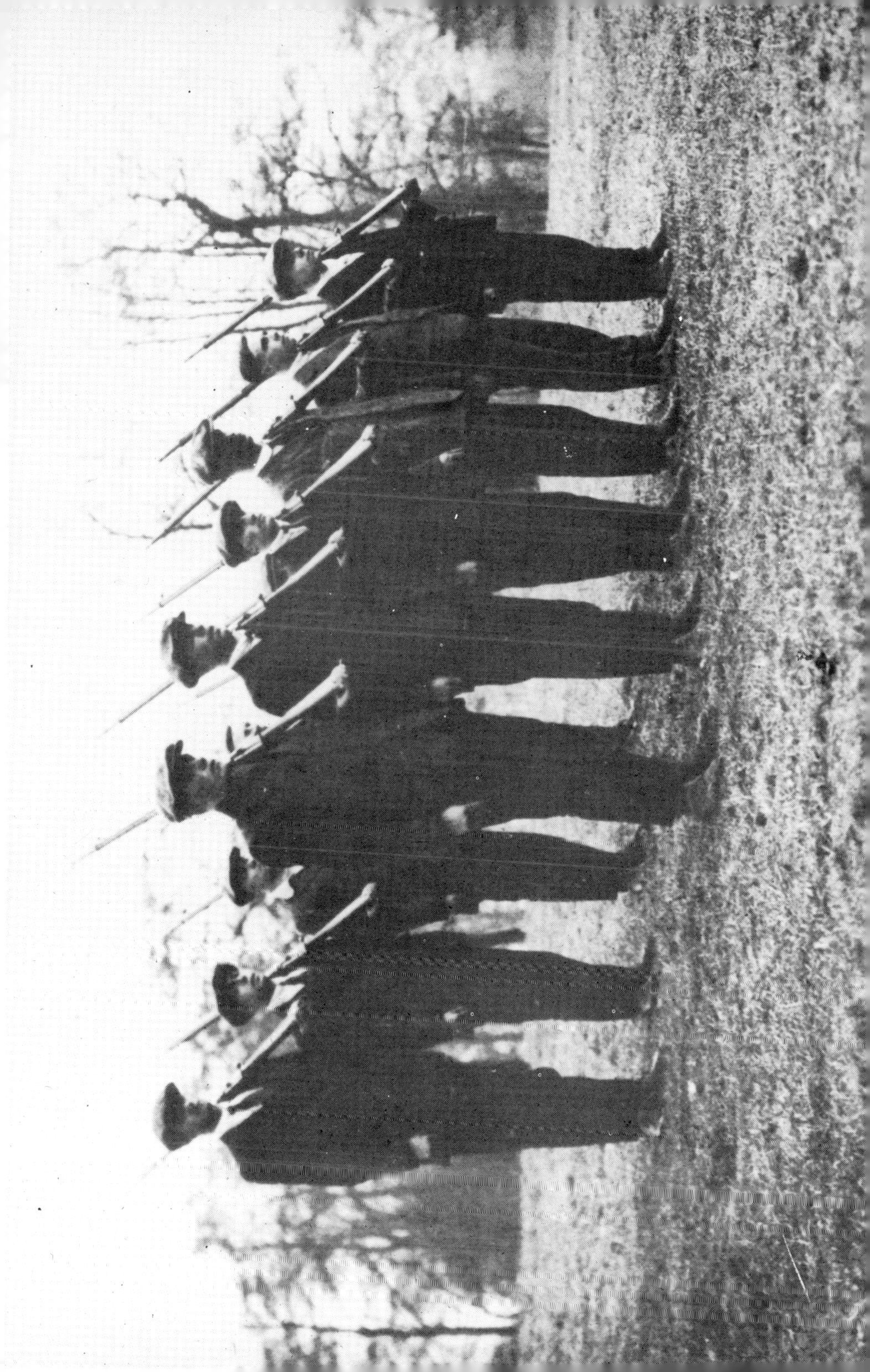

recruiting campaign was launched and in the first fortnight of 1915, well over a thousand men volunteered locally:-

January, 1915	Wigan	Atherton	Leigh
1	11	1	8
2	39	11	19
3 (Sunday)	56	0	0
4	76	26	20
5	115	40	53
6	91	29	38
7	36	16	55
8	43	6	8
9	98	8	17
10 (Sunday)	0	0	0
11	65	19	37
12	55	23	41
13	28	19	8
14	23	5	9
	736	202	413

By mid-1915, Wigan had furnished its share of recruits. In just one parish alone, St. Joseph's Roman Catholic Parish, Wigan, some 530 men were in uniform:-

Manchester Regiment	130
Lancashire Fusiliers	92
Loyal North Lancashire Regiment	82
Royal Artillery	80
Border Regiment	23
Royal Engineers	20
King's Liverpool Regiment	13
Guards	12
Army Service Corps	12
Royal Army Medical Corps	8
Royal Navy	7

while the remainder were distributed throughout a further 25 regiments.

There was no impetus for a 'pals regiment' but for those who wished to enlist together, a company of the 14/Manchester Regiment was designated 'Wigan Pals'.

Many recruits enlisted on impulse. Harry Holcroft (no relation) returned one evening to his home in Crawford Village from his job at White Moss Colliery, Skelmesdale to find a recruiting meeting in progress. Still in his black face he joined up with four others. Within six months he was in France. He had been no further than Wigan in his life. Without previous military experience this "New Army' or 'Kitchener's Army' had been training for two years but for most, this was to be their first battle. How would these thirteen divisions, over three-quarters of the army, perform in their baptism of fire?

The rank and file were reassured by the care taken in the planning of this battle by comparison to earlier assaults. Private Barton, R.A.M.C., was most impressed:-

> "The preparations were magnificent in every detail. Here is one such instance. We had a model of the German lines, roads, trenches, and all units of our division concerned in the great attack received lectures on it. Our people meant to have no mistakes this time."
> W.E. 14th. Oct., 1916

They needed to. The German position was a tough nut to crack. For almost all of its length it occupied the higher ground giving better observation for the defenders and making attack extremely difficult.

British planners saw artillery as the key to the assault. There were over 1,600 field guns, three times the number used at Loos, and the hope was that the sheer volume of gunfire would do the trick. It was assumed that the German defences would be demolished, trenches blown up, dug-outs blown in, barbed-wire entanglements destroyed and the defenders killed or stunned, so that the advancing British infantry need only walk at a leisurely pace across No-Man's-Land to occupy the enemy trenches.

This was the basic error of the British plan, an over optimistic view of the effects of the artillery combined with an unduly pessimistic opinion of the qualities of the New Army and Territorial soldiers, that they were incapable of advancing except in a slow linear formation, which exposed thousands of heavily burdened men to enemy fire for an unnecessarily long period. And burdened they were. Each man wore a steel helmet, and carried on average over 60 pounds of equipment, rifle, pack, two bandoleers of ammunition, three grenades, rations, waterproof cape, four empty sand bags, a full water bottle, pick and shovel. Some had wire-cutters. Even if they had been instructed to it would have been impossible for them to move faster that at a slow walk.

So began the heaviest bombardment yet in the history of the British army:-

Date	Shells fired
June 24	138,000
25	139,000
26	212,000
27	236,000
28	168,000
28	190,000
30	375,000
July 1	224,000

Private Darby wrote home to his parents in Plank Lane, Leigh:-

> "The bombardment continued day and night and how the Germans stuck it God only knows."
> L.J.. 28th. July, 1916

With one field gun to every twenty yards of front including one heavy artillery piece for every sixty yards, over one and three quarter million shells pounded the German lines during the eight day bombardment, seventy shells for every yard of defences. Some idea of the bombardment's intensity is given in the Regimental History of the 27th. (Wurtenburg) Division:-

> "What we experienced surpassed all previous conception. The enemy's fire never ceased for an hour. It fell day and night on the

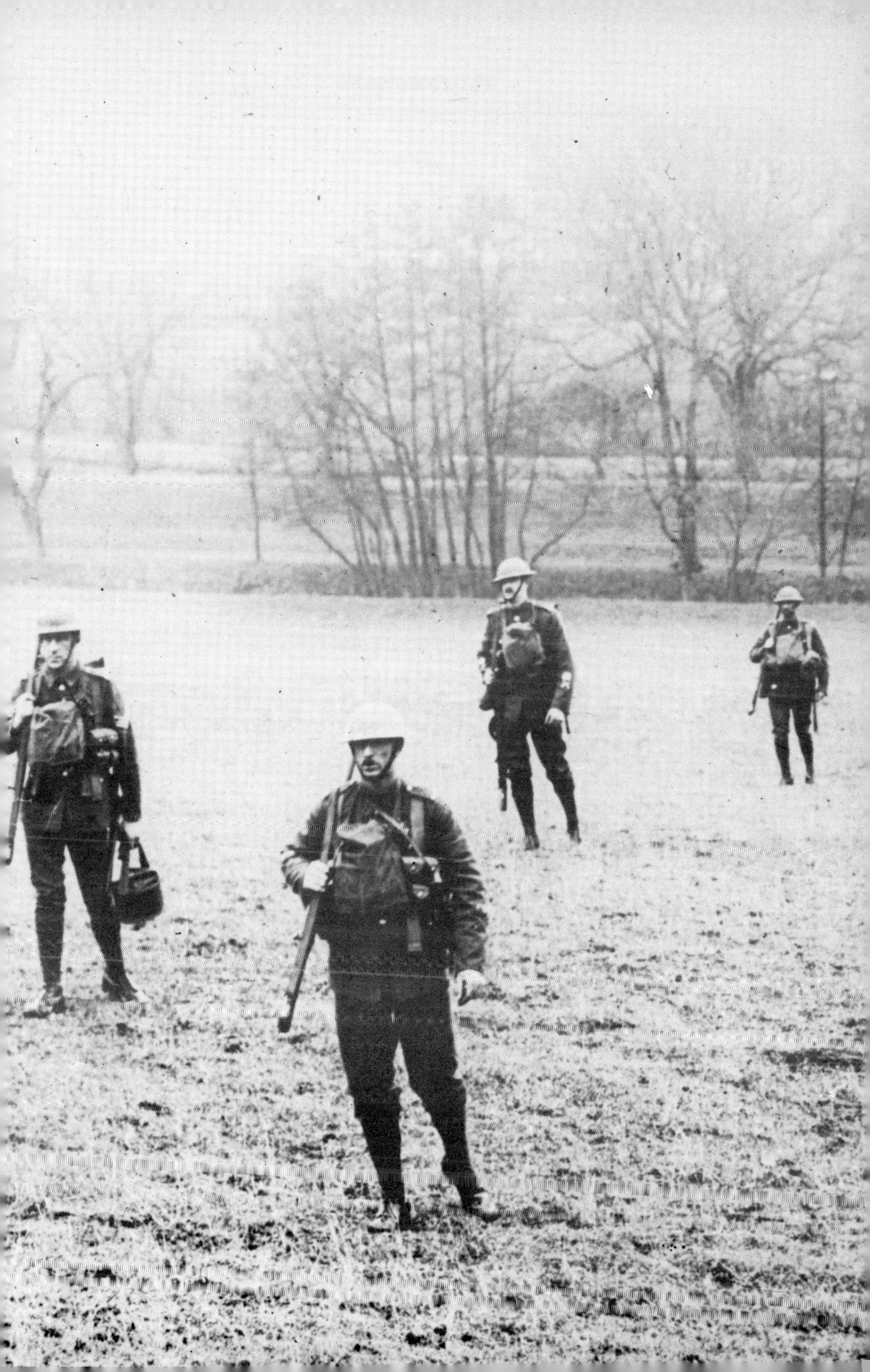

front line and tore fearful gaps in the ranks of the defenders. It fell on the approaches to the front and made all movement towards the front line hell. It fell on the rearward trenches and on the battery positions and smashed men and material in a manner never seen before."

The British badly needed to know the state of the German barbed-wire and during several nights from the 24th. to the 30th. June, they sent out raiding parties to gather information. During the night of the 28th./29th. June, Corporal Fred Belshaw of the Oxford and Buckinghamshire Regiment, son of the headmaster of Top Lane Church of England School, Tyldesley, was caught in the barbed-wire while taking part in such activities and knocked unconscious. His small party carried him back through No-Man's-Land in the darkness by following a tape they had laid on their outward journey. This, like similar raids, brought back disappointing news. The wire had not been damaged by the artillery as much as had been hoped.

Private Tom Smith wrote to his parents in Wigan describing what it felt like to take part in a trench raid:-

> "the order came 'off tunics' and we went over the top in our shirt sleeves with rifles, bayonets, and bombs. When the order came 'over' we all jumped up as one man, We darted through our wire where we had cut a gap the night before then we laid down in the grass in silence while we got in proper order. Then we began to creep a little nearer to their wire. What a sensation. With the thunderous noise of the guns and the lights sent up by the enemy. But we got nearer and our wire-cutters began to cut a gap through their defences. As soon as we got the word 'wire clear' we were not long before we were through into their trenches. Our lads cleared them with bombs. I was in charge of the 'looting section', that is to say going into the dug-outs and getting all we could carry back. We dropped on several of the enemy in a dug-out. They would not come out so one of our bombers let them have a couple of bombs (hand-grenades). I don't think they could have come out even if they had wanted to after that. Any way we brought nine prisoners back with us. One was an officer but I believe he died. Then came the time to withdraw. We did it very well and we only had four casualties. We rushed into our

trenches and when everyone was in we shook hands and cheered with joy."
W.E. 11th. July, 1916.

Not so lucky was Lieutenant Lawrence Bloy of the Lancashire Fusiliers, a relative of Francis Sharpe-Powell (Wigan's best known M.P.), who led a trench raid on the eve of the attack. His friend Captain Hutchinson wrote later that when they reached the German trenches hand-to-hand fighting broke out where Bloy:-

'was attacked by four Germans, an officer and three men who he knocked down with the butt of his rifle. I was distracted and when I looked round he had disappeared."
W.O. 13th. Feb., 1917.

Posted missing in action, Bloy was only officially declared dead when his name appeared on a list supplied by the Germans six months later. Another local officer was lost in the same raid. Lieutenant Harold Ainscow from Hindley was also posted as missing but two months later he turned up wounded in a Bavarian hospital.

On the eve of the battle, confidence was high in the British trenches. Six months earlier Private Glover of Fogg's Fold, Platt Bridge had written home:-

"All out here are in the highest spirits, I can assure the 'slackers' that they will never know what the word 'manhood' means until they are behind the parapet with 200 rounds of ammunition and a trusty rifle and bayonet. We are all as game as ever and never grumble because we know we are fighting for a good cause."
W.O. 11th. December, 1915.

A week of concentrated shelling was considered sufficient and at exactly 7.30 a.m. on the morning of 1st. July, 1916, the bombardment suddenly ceased and the battlefield fell silent.

MAP 3: THE SOMME BATTLEFIELD, 1st JULY 1916.

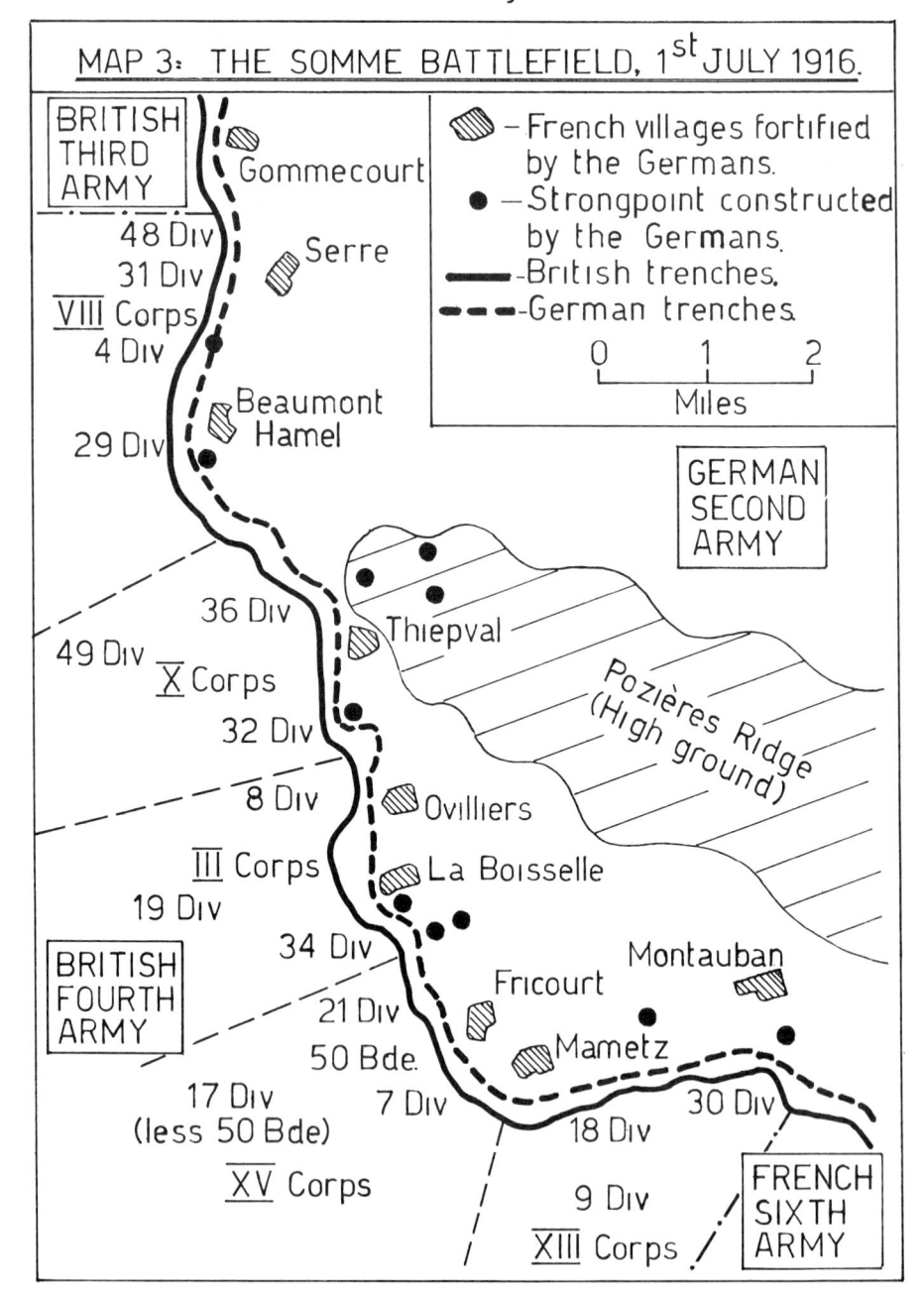

CHAPTER II The Attack.

Seconds later whistles blew, officers shouted encouragement and in response, the long khaki lines rose from the earth and moved forward. Private Thomas Edwin Walker of the York and Lancaster Regiment of 4, The Hillock, Blackamoor, Astley in a letter to his family gave some indication of the men's feelings in those last moments before going over the top:-

"Just before the order to charge, I saw a mental vision of each of your faces and the next moment I was in a mass of yelling, cursing men with no thought of anything but to kill."
L.J. 14th. July, 1916.

Private Ingram, normally a coal miner at Abram Colliery, wrote home to Hindley:-

"We advanced over the top at 7.30 in the morning. About five minutes before, word was passed down to load our rifles and fix our bayonets and then the whistle went to go over. All the officers wished us luck on the journey. As soon as we got through our own barbed-wire the Germans started their artillery and machine-guns. All the boys were cool and walked as if going to a picnic. The shells were bursting around us and bullets too."
W.O. 20th. July, 1916.

Before they could open out into their attacking formations, the British infantry had first to negotiate their own barbed-wire through lanes cut by the engineers during the previous night. It was then that some units received their first shock. In places the artillery barrage had not totally destroyed the German defences and along the eighteen mile front, the defenders were in varying stages of readiness. Some were quick enough to fire as the British soldiers filed through the narrow paths in their own barbed-wire defences.

Out in the open, lines of men moved forward steadily, rifles with bayonets fixed held diagonally across their chests. After crouching in their trenches and dug-outs for several days passively enduring the terrible British bombardment they called 'trummel feur' (drumfire), the Germans emerged from below ground as the British infantry advanced towards them out in the open at an unbelievably slow pace. Casualties mounted as German machine-guns began their ominous chatter, sweeping backwards and forwards, left and right, cutting down men in swathes, and leaving long rows of dead and wounded on the ground. Attackers fell in their droves but there was no panic among the survivors, training and discipline maintained their progress.

After a few minutes, the German artillery added its contribution to the defence. Shells screamed vertically downwards across the centre of No-Man's-Land, raising a symmetrical line of vivid explosions each with its plume of black smoke through which the advancing infantry had to penetrate. Hit early in the attack, Private Walker had to lie motionless in No-Man's-Land watching horrified:-

> "I saw some awful sights. Young lads blown to atoms."
> L.J. 14th. July, 1916.

A German eyewitness paid tribute to the qualities of the ordinary British soldier:-

> "A series of extended lines of infantry were seen moving forward from the British trenches. The first line appeared to continue without end to right and left. It was quickly followed by a second line, then a third and fourth. They came out at a steady pace as if expecting to find nothing alive in our front trenches.
> The front line, preceded by a thin line of skirmishers and bombers was now halfway across No-Man's-Land. When the leading British line was within a hundred yards, the rattle of machine-guns and rifle fire broke out along our whole line. Rockets signalled to the artillery and immediately shells from batteries in the rear burst among the advancing lines.
> Whole sections seemed to fall and the rear formations moving in closer order quickly scattered. The advance rapidly crumpled under this hail of shell and bullets. All along the line men could be seen throwing up their arms and collapsing, never to move again. Badly wounded rolled about in agony while less severely injured crawled to the nearest shell-hole for safety.

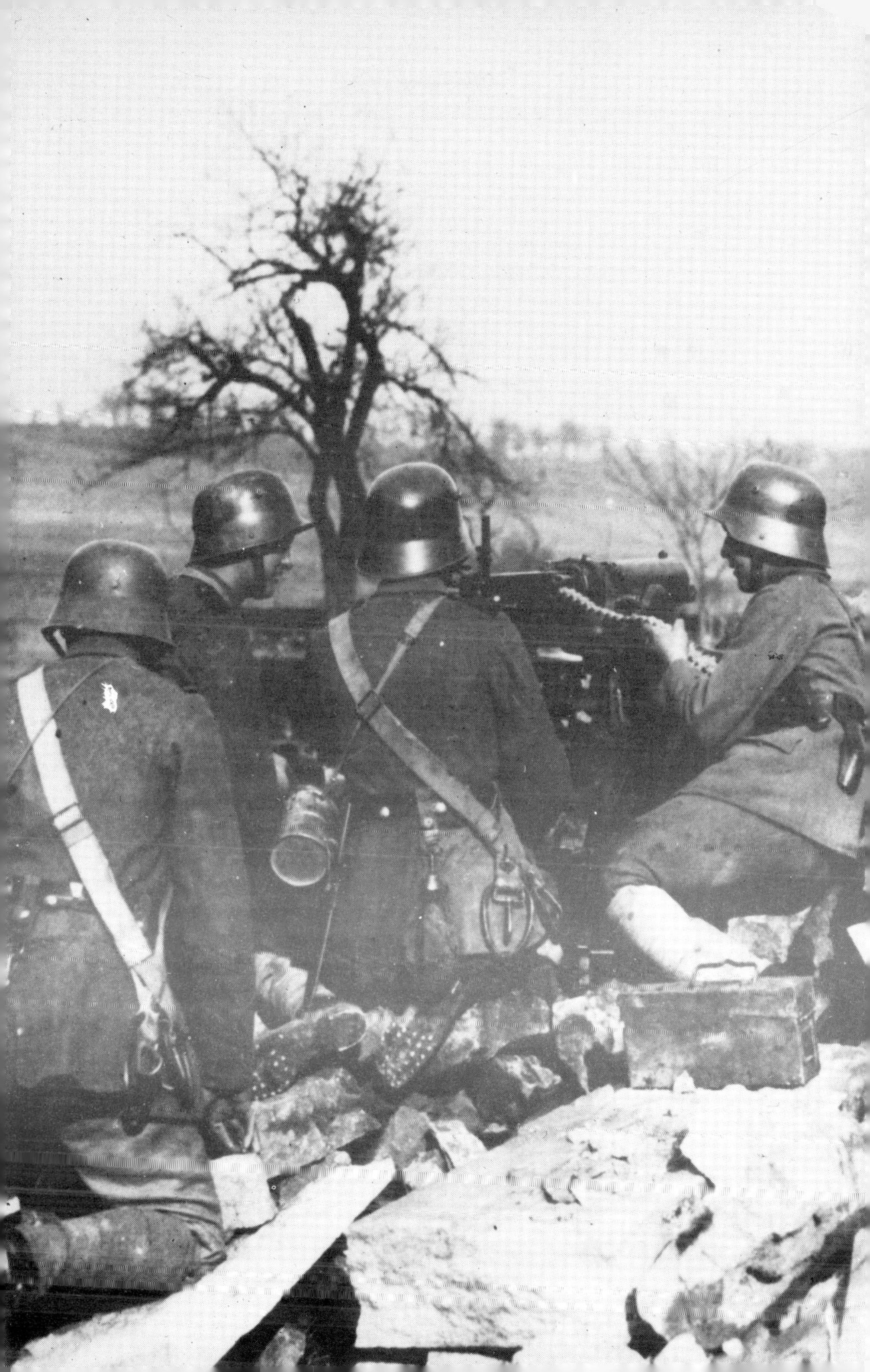

The British soldier, however, has no lack of courage. The extended lines, though badly shaken and with many gaps now came on all the faster. Instead of a leisurely walk they covered the ground in short rushes at the double. Within a few minutes the leading troops had advanced to within a stone's throw of our trench and while some of us continued to fire at point blank range, others threw hand-grenades. British bombers answered back while others rushed forward with fixed bayonets. Again and again the extended lines of British infantry broke against the German defence, like waves against a cliff only to be beaten back. It was an amazing spectacle of unexampled gallantry, courage and bulldog determination."

Along parts of the line, particularly where they had left their own trenches early before the British barrage had stopped, the first attack wave quickly reached the German trenches where they expected to find the barbed-wire destroyed by the artillery. In places the wire was indeed blown away, elsewhere it was only damaged although still passable with difficulty and in both instances the attackers scrambled through, but in many places the British received a second shock, the wire was completely undamaged. Further heavy losses were incurred as the defenders fired point blank on the British soldiers entangled in the wire. Despite this, the attackers penetrated the wire defences in several places and vicious hand-to-hand fighting with bayonets and hand-grenades broke out in the German positions.

Within half an hour, one third of the first line of German trenches at the southern end of the battlefield had been captured, along another third of the line, mainly in the centre, small isolated pockets of German first-line trenches had been taken, but in the northern sector no attacker had even reached the nearest German positions. Losses had been horrific, half the first wave were killed or wounded, thirty thousand men were already casualties.

It was now time for the supporting waves to follow. Where the leading wave had broken into the German trenches, defensive machine-gun fire had slackened enough to allow considerable numbers to cross No-Man's-Land in support but where the defenders had held out, reinforcements were mown down by a withering machine-gun fire. Where the first wave had moved on without properly 'mopping up' German survivors in the first trench, following waves were fired on by Germans emerging from their deep dug-outs. Where the first wave had been repulsed the second wave stood no chance. It too was obliterated.

Everywhere the supports entered a nightmare world where, through the dust and noise of explosions, amid the whizz of bullets and the clatter of machine-guns, they had to step over the dead and dying bodies of their comrades lying singly and in heaps across their path. Towards them staggered or crawled the shell-shocked and wounded survivors of the first wave. Already the timetable for the second wave battalions had gone horribly wrong yet they were still being sent forward. All that this achieved were more lines of dead and more streams of walking wounded making their way to the rear for treatment. Many survivors could only take cover in the shell-holes and craters of No-Man's-Land with the remnants of the leading wave. The British artillery had moved closer to the front line in a vain effort to give added support, first to 5,000 yards and so close at 1,000 yards that they were in danger of being captured and casualties mounted among the gunners and drivers. Bombardier William Richardson, R.F.A., from Poostock Lane was among those killed. His friend, Signaller Reaney wrote home:-

> "We had to lay a wire from our first line of trenches after the infantry made the charge. Bill, an officer and myself, mounted the parapet with the telephone wire. We had gone about eighty yards when poor Bill put up his arms and fell like a ton weight into a shell hole. I turned round to look at him but I couldn't stop long, I had to follow my officer. We had gone anther five yards when the officer was wounded twice. He crawled into the hole where Bill was and I went myself to see what I could do but it was no use. Shells were bursting all around. It was hell on earth."
> W.E. 25th. July, 1916.

He did what he could for them but both men later died of their wounds.

Only a few months earlier many of these soldiers had been civilians working as coal miners, clerks and shop assistants, What they saw was beyond anything they might have expected, Private Hector of the Border Regiment:-

"No human being could forget it in a lifetime."
W.E. 14th. Oct., 1916.

Private Barton, also from Wigan, was similarly affected:-

"The night before saw us standing-to in our trenches. The suspense was terrible, it told on many chap's nerves, especially the intense fire of the last few hours. My section had to go over the top into No-Man's-Land to bring back the wounded. We got the order to go over and the reception we got I shall never forget. It was terrible. We had not even a sporting chance. At this time the battle developed into an inferno. It was simply raining with shrapnel and bullets were singing everywhere. I consider myself lucky to get out alive."
W.E. 14th. Oct., 1916.

Now occurred that most feared of all war-time disasters, a breakdown in communications between the front line and headquarters. Although they could see what was happening to their men, the battalion commanders lost contact with them. Field telegraph wires were constantly cut by shellfire, flags and lamps proved useless as their operators were shot the moment they exposed themselves and runners risked almost certain death every time they zig-zagged across No-Man's-Land with a message. Fifty battalion commanders disobeyed orders to remain in the British trenches and went forward to help. Thirty were killed. The orderly set-piece battle which had been so carefully planned over so many months now disintegrated into hundreds of separate individual actions as tiny groups of survivors battled for their lives.

Medical personnel worked tirelessly and heroically among the wounded. Private James Gregory, R.A.M.C. of 35, Chapel Green, Hindley, attached to the Northumberland Fusiliers was hit by a shellburst while carrying a wounded man to the doctor's dug-out and

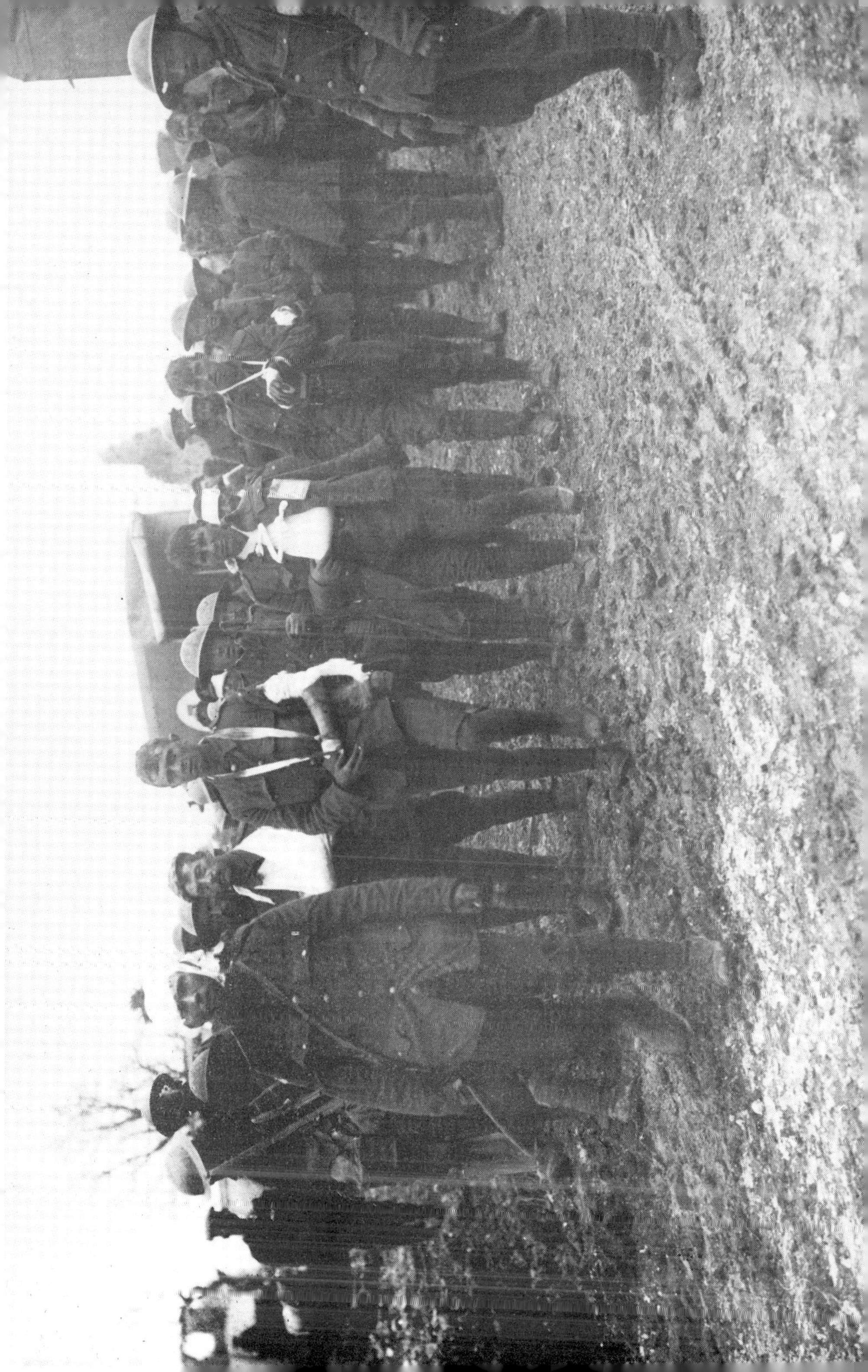

was awarded the Military Medal. Another R.A.M.C. man, William Aldred, of Cambridge Street, Atherton, in civilian life a collier at Fletcher Burrows' Arley Mine and treasurer of the local Salvation Army branch was given the D.C.M. for his bravery fetching in wounded men under heavy fire. Several R.A.M.C. men were killed as they recklessly exposed themselves, Thomas Smith of Leigh and William Young of Golborne, both attached to the Gordon Highlanders, and Arthur Yates from Wigan, attached to the King's Royal Rifles among them.

The plight of the wounded was terrible. Sapper Edwards of the Royal Engineers was one of the lucky ones:-

> "I made my way back after having my wound dressed and threaded my way through the thick of my comrades who lay dead and some helpless waiting for the stretcher bearers to bring them to safety."
> L.J. 21st. July.

Driver Kennett from Tyldesley in the Royal Field Artillery wrote home of seeing some dreadful scenes:-

> "The trenches are full of dead and dying and some of them have been thirty hours waiting for attention. Ambulances are running at full speed and everybody is doing their best. I have seen over a hundred bodies in one line waiting to be buried."
> L.J. 14th. July, 1916.

Private Houghton of 1/Lancashire Fusiliers from 67, Trafalgar Street, Leigh, wounded in the leg and unable to move was missing for two days before being found. Lance Corporal Fred Wright wrote home to Ashton-in-Makerfield where, before the war he had assisted in his father's grocery shop. Half way across No-Man's-Land he had been hit in the right leg by a machine-gun bullet:-

> "The bullet had gone clean through the leg. I lay in a dip in the ground to take cover from the Germans who were sweeping the area with machine-gun bullets, There were also one or two snipers who, when our wounded tried to move away, they

'popped them off'. I was wounded about 8.30 a.m. An hour later I was hit by a sniper about three inches away from the first wound. I had used all my dressing bandages and had none for my second wound. However I took off my puttee and tied it tightly round the top of my leg to stop the bleeding. By this time it was getting hot with shells and shrapnel and I spotted a shell hole so I crawled to it pulling myself along with my hands and left leg. I did not stay there long because I was constantly being covered by dirt kicked up by shell bursts all around me! I then crawled back over one hundred and twenty yards through shell holes, past men who could not move, and finally through our barbed-wire. This was a terrible job on one's stomach because your clothes got entangled with the spikes on the wire."
W.O. 29th. July, 1916.

Wright dropped, exhausted, into a shallow trench,. After lying there for twenty four hours he had not been attended to so he attempted to crawl to the dressing station on his own but collapsed. He lay for a further twenty four hours before being found and taken for treatment.

Private Ton Schofield, who in civilian life had worked at the Lancashire and Yorkshire Railway's goods depot in Wigan, wrote home to 126, Poolstock Lane. Hit by shrapnel in both thighs, breaking his right leg, he crawled into a shell hole just in front of the German trenches. When his regiment retreated he hopped along with them before throwing himself into a trench. Next day the walking wounded went to the field dressing station but it was the 4th. July before the stretcher bearers found him:-

"The worst thing I had to undergo was thirst., I managed to get two water bottles but they had gone in the first two days. The third day there was a good shower of rain and I caught the water in a ground sheet and filled the bottles. I was very careful with it. With the ground being very soft I sank two feet and couldn't get out of it. But it was a fine day the day after and I got pretty dry. When I got to the dressing station I got some hot milk and I didn't half give it socks!"
W.O. 29th. July, 1916.

As the hot, dusty summer day wore on with blue cloudless skies overhead, the battlefield slowly quietened. Where the British had been successful, they sank exhausted to the ground. Where they had been unsuccessful, tragedy stalked. Between the two lines of trenches, all was silent, the stillness now and again punctuated by the odd rifle crack. When darkness fell an amazing transformation took place as No-Man's-Land suddenly came alive. Thousands of wounded British soldiers who had endured hours of silent agony, terribly injured but forced to lie perfectly still, not daring to stir for fear of attracting the enemy's fire, decided that it was now time to move. Those who were not so close to the German lines that they were captured, crawled, limped or staggered back to their own trenches. Some never made it.

The first day on the Somme was over. It had been a disaster.

MAP 4: GROUND GAINED – 1st JULY 1916.

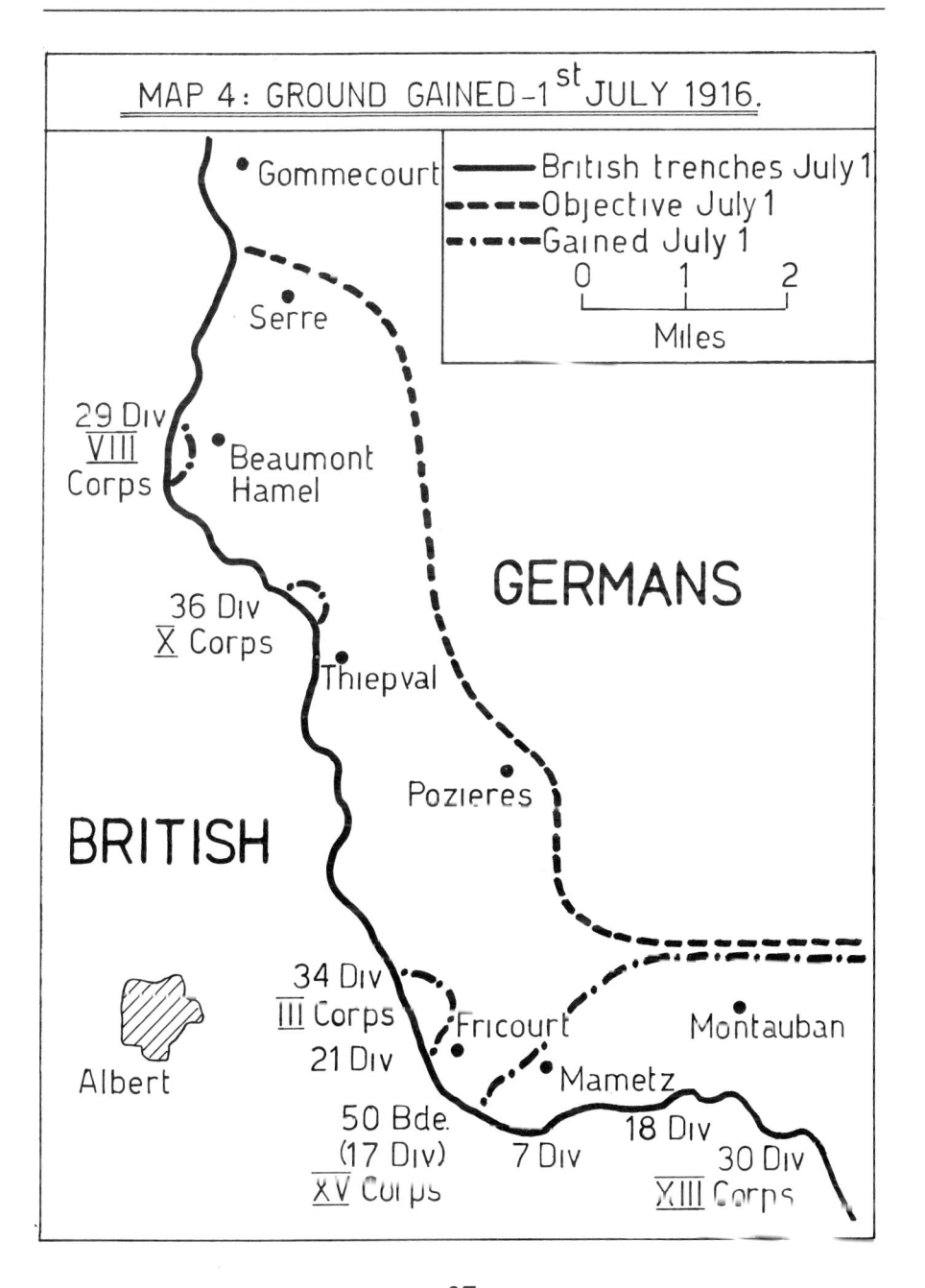

CHAPTER III Casualties.

When the rolls were called next morning, almost 62,000 men were casualties.

	Killed	Wounded	Missing	Total
Officers	721	1,531	339	2,591
Men	7,449	34,357	17,419	59,225
				61,816

Subsequently most of the missing were accounted for. A few re-appeared or were reported taken prisoner but most swelled the numbers of those killed. The revised figures were:-

	Killed[1]	Wounded	Missing	Total
Officers	993	1,337	96	2,438
Men	18,247	34,156	2,056	55,032
				57,470

Altogether, 21,392 men were lost on the most disastrous day in the history of the British Army, most of them in the first hour. In return for this mindless massacre of the finest manhood of Great Britain, the veteran regulars of the Old Army and the enthusiastic volunteers of the New Army, there was precious little to show on the ground.

Soon the hospitals were crowded with the wounded survivors. Within a month 15,000 wounded soldiers filled to overflowing the military and auxiliary hospitals around Manchester where the medical staff worked round the clock. This scenario was repeated in cities across the country. Because many New Army battalions had been recruited on a local basis and the territorials had agreed to serve overseas, these terrible losses were concentrated on particular areas, especially in the northern industrial towns where so many enthusiastic, patriotic recruits had volunteered in 1914.

The most poignant losses were among the 'pals battalions' where groups of friends, neighbours, and workmates had enlisted together,

[1]*Including, 'died of wounds'.*

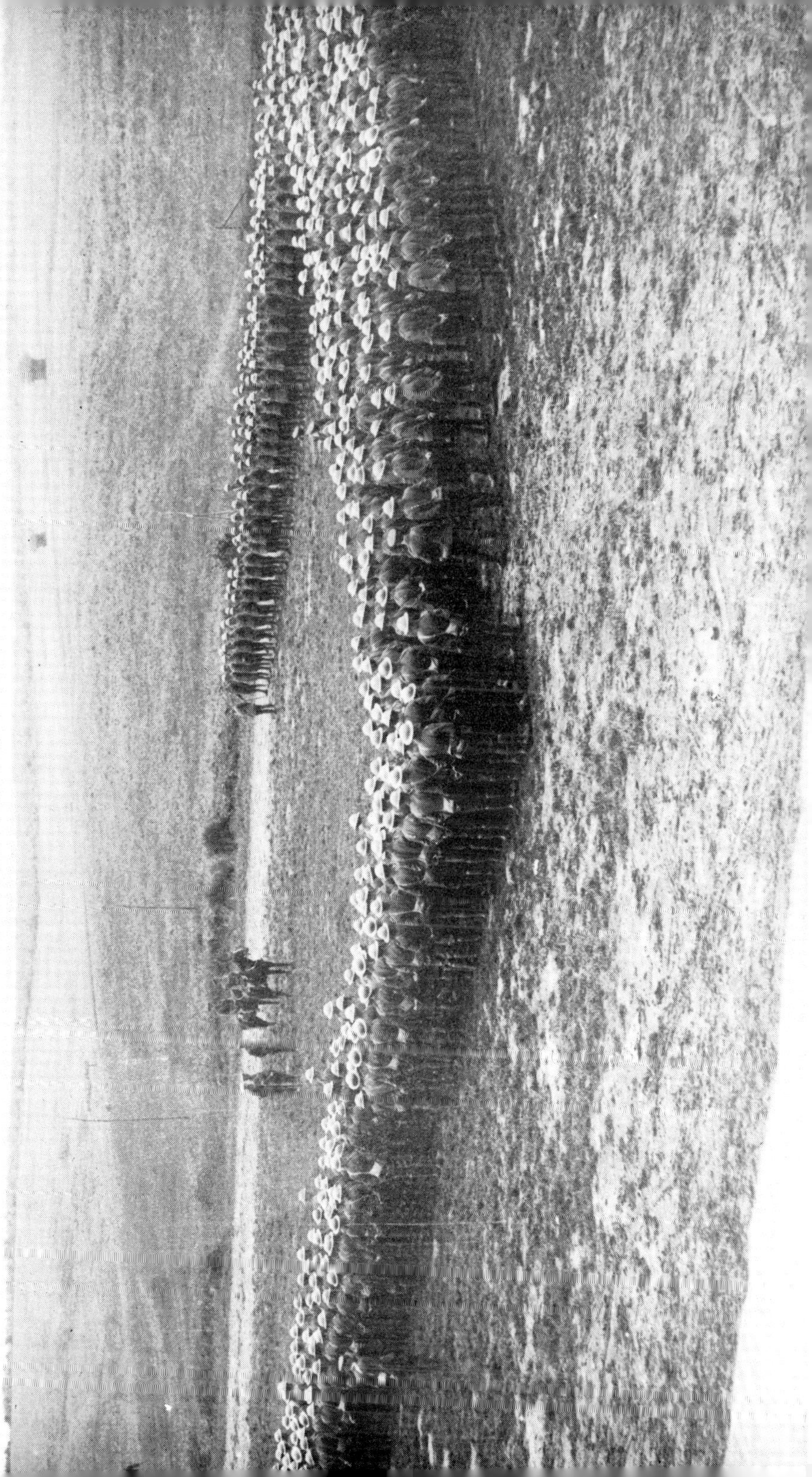

the Accrington Pals, Bradford Pals, Glasgow Boy's Brigade Battalion, five battalions of Tyneside Pals and in its own way a pals' battalion, the Newfoundland Regiment, each suffered over five hundred casualties.

The lists of killed and wounded and missing seemed endless, filling page after page of 'The Times' and 'The Manchester Guardian'. To read out all the names would have taken two weeks. Telegrams bringing the dreaded news that their loved ones were either killed or missing arrived at homes in every city, town and hamlet across the country. In some towns it seemed as if every street received at least one, sometimes two telegrams. How people were affected locally, in the Leigh district, has been movingly described in Evelyn Finch's book 'Leigh and the Somme', so that will not be repeated here. Sometimes a letter from a comrade arrived before the official telegram. When Fred Briscoe was killed on 1st. July, 1916, his friend Private Joseph Norovice wrote almost apologetically to Briscoe's home in Leigh:-

> "I was one of the lucky ones that came through it. I carried him back on a stretcher and thought it right to look through his pockets for the address of his parents so I might inform you."
> L.J. 21st. July, 1916.

Letters usually stressed that the deceased soldier had been bravely doing his duty and that the end had been quick and painless. Following an immense rise in the numbers of recipients. War Pensions, particularly for those disabled by their wounds, were upgraded. Viewed in print they look as cold and unfeeling as the bureaucrats who worked out the weekly payments:-

Loss of Leg		Loss of Arm	
up to the hip	18/-	right arm to shoulder	16/-
at the thigh	14/-	left arm to shoulder	15/-
above the knee	12/6d.	above the right elbow	13/-
below the knee	10/6d.	above the left elbow	11/6d.
		below the right elbow	11/6d.
		below the left elbow	10/6d.

Not much, and small compensation for men who had formerly held jobs demanding a high degree of physical exertion in the mines, factories and mills, on the railways and on the land. There was little sympathy for left-handers! Widows' and dependants' pensions were also augmented:-

Widow of:-	age under 35	age 35-44	age 45 plus
Sergeant	11/	13/6	16/-
Corporal	10/6	13/-	15/6
Private	10/-	12/6	15/-

In addition mothers received 5/- a week for the first child, 3/6d. for the second child and 2/- for the third and any subsequent children. Not a lot. Already the British Red Cross and the St. John's Ambulance were spending £34,000 weekly across the country on the families of dead and wounded soldiers.

The bereaved were in desperate need of comfort. The local clergy worked tirelessly but were overwhelmed by the demands on their services. They too had suffered grievously. After two years of war, the Vicar of Haigh had lost all four sons and the Rector of Pemberton had lost both his. In response to the innumerable cries for aid the Salvation Army set up a nationwide network of Widows' Counsellors with the intention to *'place within the reach of widows needing assistance the services of sympathetic and practical advisors who will help them with their affairs and guide them in their difficulties.'* The local branch was kept busy.

Those left behind needed plenty of help with their everyday affairs. Inflation was pushing up the cost of even the most basic everyday items, especially food. Since the outbreak of the war, the price of 5lb of potatoes had risen from 2d. to 8d., a pound of flour from 1d. to 2d., a pound of butter from 1/- to 2/- a pound of beef from 10d. to 1/5d. and a hundredweight of coal from 11d. to 1/4d.

Most bereaved families suffered silently and the full force of the horrendous losses defies imagination, but the impact is amply illustrated by the story of just one casualty Harry Entwistle, a Kitchener volunteer in the 22nd. Battalion of the Manchester

Regiment. Before the war he had been a booking clerk and telegrapher, first at Ince station then at Hindley station for the Lancashire and Yorkshire Railway Company. Harry was a staunch Anglican while his fiancé, Winnie Gore from Platt Bridge was a devout Roman Catholic and in those more intolerant times their pre-war romance should have been doomed but it had only drawn both families together. On hearing of Harry's death on 1st. July, 1916, Winnie withdrew from society and entered a convent from which she never emerged for the rest of her life. Almost fifty years later, sometime in 1960, Winnie sent a verbal message through a relative, who by a strange coincidence was a workmate of Harry's nephew and namesake, passing on regards to the Entwistle family adding that it was from:-

"your Auntie Winnie who died long ago with Uncle Harry."

Multiply this incident by the total losses on that fateful day and some idea can be gleaned of the impact of the Somme offensive on the people of Great Britain. Despite losing over a hundred local men killed on the opening day of the Battle of the Somme, the district was spared the traumas suffered in other towns when news of the casualties among the pals' battalions filtered back. Wigan and Leigh had already been shaken by the losses of their local territorials, the 1/5 Manchester Regiment, in the Dardenelles during 1915 but luckily escaped the concentrated casualties of the 1st. July, 1916. Territorial and New Army battalions containing large numbers of local men were not involved on the opening day of the battle and with the exception of the Lancashire Fusiliers and the Border Regiment, career soldiers from this locality were spread thinly among the British Army's regular regiments. Still, as the Appendix shows, over one hundred local men lost their lives on the 1st. July, 1916 making it the worst day of the war for this district. The sheer size of the figures numbs the mind. Every Corps and Division has its own story to tell.

CHAPTER IV   Corps Attacks.

XIII CORPS.
XIII Corps held the southern or right flank of the Fourth Army, Theirs was the only corps to achieve all of their first day objectives although the British trenches lay near the bottom of the valley side and the German front-line was higher up the slope so that the XIII Corps had to attack uphill.

30 Division.
This was the first battle for nine New Army battalions recruited from the Manchester and Liverpool districts, so containing many local men, stiffened by four regular battalions.

Brigade	Battalion	Type	Origin
21st	18/ King's Liverpool	New Army	2/Liverpool Pals
	19/Manchester	New Army	4/Manchester Pals
	2/Wiltshire	Regulars	
	2/Green Howards	Regulars	
89th.	17/King's Liverpool	New Army	1/Liverpool Pals
	19/King's Liverpool	New Army	3/Liverpool Pals
	20/King's Liverpool	New Army	4/Liverpool Pals
	2/Bedford Regiment	Regulars	
90th	16/Manchester	New Army	1/Manchester Pals
	17/Manchester	New Army	2/Manchester Pals
	18/Manchester	New Army	3/Manchester Pals
	2/Royal Scots	Regulars	
Pioneers	11/South Lancashire	New Army	St. Helens Pals

On the right, the 1st. and 4th. Liverpool Pals crossed No-Man's-Land in quick time, overran the German front line and pushed ahead with few casualties, On their left the 2nd. Liverpool Pals and the 4th. Manchester Pals were similarly successful but with heavier casualties due to enfilade machine-gun fire, but within an hour, 30 Division's first objective had been won. With a four to one superiority over the defenders the British artillery had done its work well, reducing the German trenches to 'heaps of chalk'. When the British soldiers examined the deep German defences in detail they were amazed at what they found, Private Joseph Whaif of the South Lancashire Regiment took a close look:-

"They say the Germans are starving but they left a lot of good food behind them and loaves were in big piles. Also we found a lot of champagne and perrier water and tins of soup and beef. Their trenches are such works of engineering, some of them being forty feet below ground. The walls were papered and all kinds of musical instruments were lying about."
L.J. 14th. July, 1916.

Private McDonald confirmed this and added:-

"All his dug-outs were deep and roomy. Most of them were provided with stoves and tables while many had electric lights and speaking tubes."
W.O. 29th. July, 1916.

Many infantry crossed No-Man's-Land relatively unscathed because they used 'saps', tunnels dug by their pioneers from their front line underneath No-Man's-Land and surfacing near the German defences. The division's pioneers, 11th. South Lancashires, were coal miners and glassworkers from St. Helens Lance-Corporal Lee was one of the unsung heroes who had created these features and wrote home proudly describing:-

'the fine work done making saps from the British trenches to within thirty to forty yards from the Hun trenches, After the saps were completed the topsoil, about eighteen inches, was taken off and a small trench connected with it. This marvellous piece of work was completed in one night and without even one casualty. Imagine Fritz's surprise when he woke up on the 1st. July and found another British trench under his nose."
W.E. 1st. Aug., 1916.

Private Michael Nolan from Wigan took part in the charge.

"The bombardment was terrible. I experienced the Lancashire Landing at Gallipoli and that was from forty battleships. It only lasted an hour but at the time it seemed awful. But in this lot I think there were more shells in five minutes than were fired at Gallipolli in three months. We waited for the bombardment to

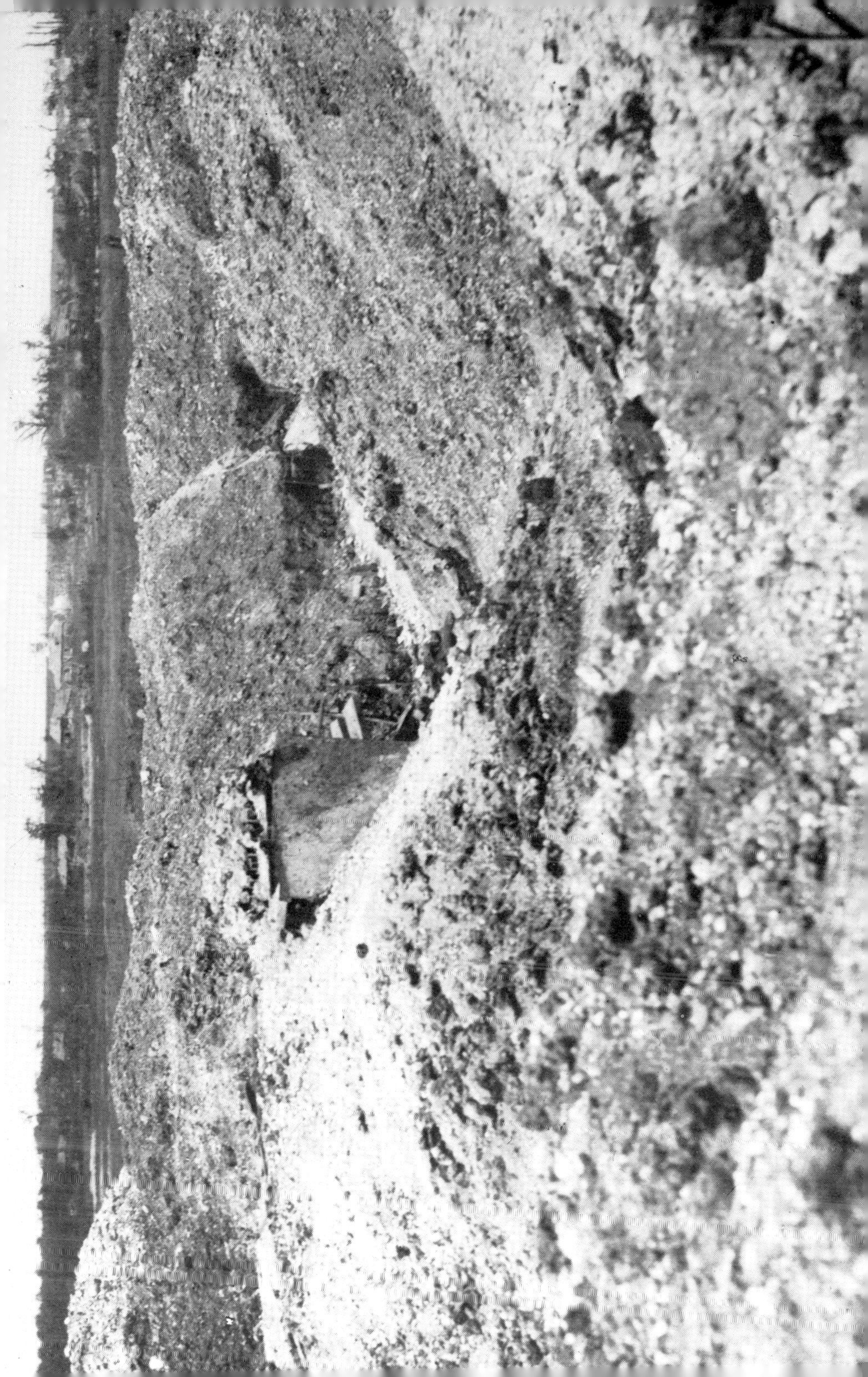

stop which it did eight days later. Then we went over the top of our trench. It seemed a walk-over for us but Fritz does not put a gun in the window he has to sell. As soon as we were within forty yards of their trenches, their machine-guns let go. They put a lot of casualties up for us but they were mostly slight wounds, Within fifteen minutes we had their first three lines of trenches from them. We took seven hundred and seventy prisoners to the rear, most of them wounded, some mad."

As the first wave paused to reorganise, three more battalions, 1st and 2nd. Manchester Pals with the 2nd. Royal Scots Fusiliers, continued the advance towards the second objective, the village of Montauban, This time the entire advance was held up again by a single machine-gun which caused immense casualties until silenced. Private Harry O'Neil, an 18 year old from 38, Sportsman Street, Leigh lost a leg in this incident:-

"As we advanced we lost heavily. As a fellow got wounded the Germans kept firing at him. I threw about eight bombs when a shell burst behind me and I was hit. Later I had to have my leg amputated."
L.J. 28th. July, 1916.

Second Lieutenant Ernest Vernon Speakman aged only 22 won the Military Cross for, as the citation reads:-

"holding his ground in the open under heavy fire of all kinds with only a few men. He shot four of the enemy himself and set a fine example."

An old boy of Leigh Grammar School, Rossall School and Wigan Mining and Technical College, he was the son of the owner of Bedford Colliery. The Official History of the War speaks admirably of the second wave:-

"The advance of the Manchesters was carried out with remarkable steadiness and enthusiasm in spite of severe casualties."

The Finest of All

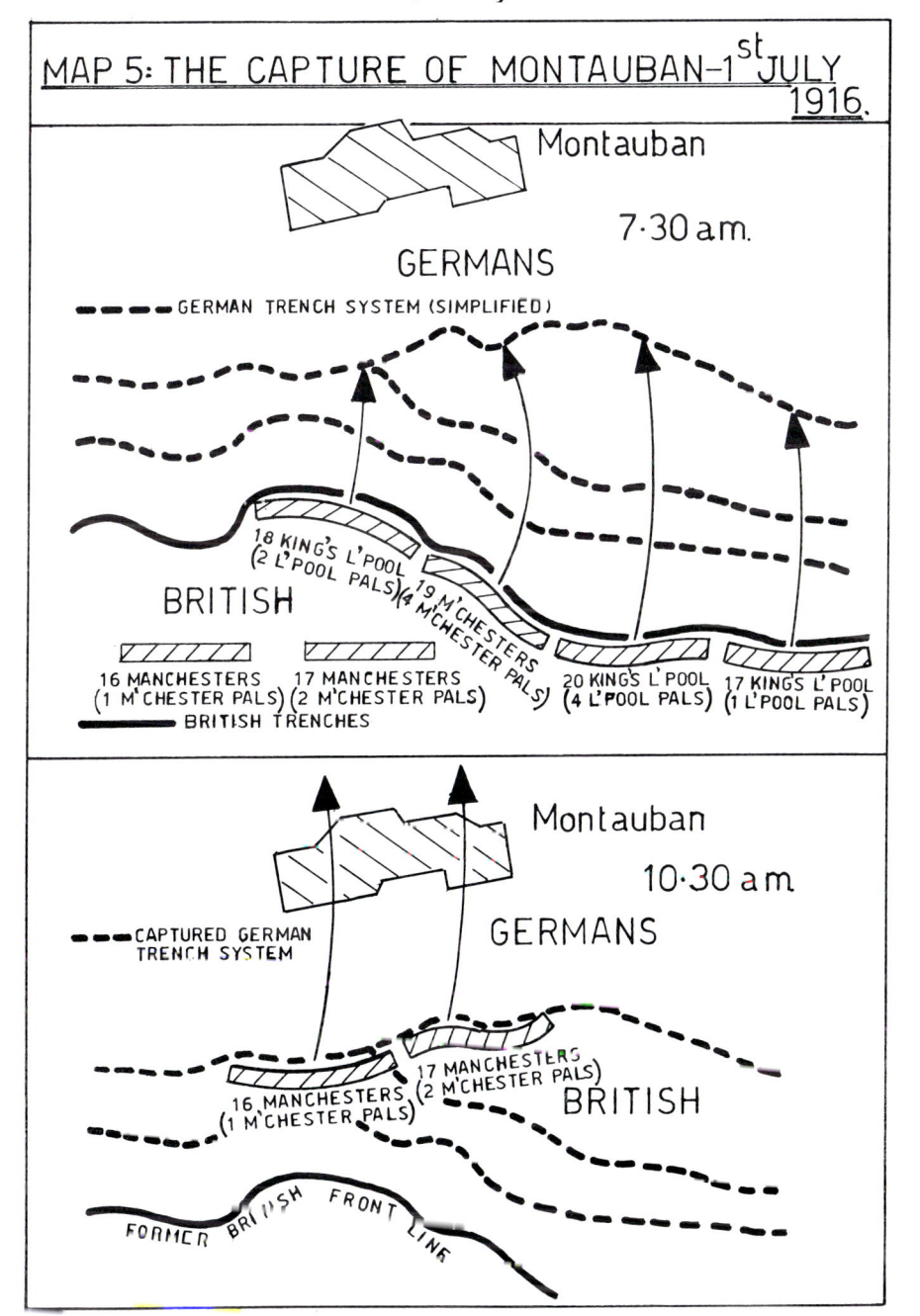

MAP 5: THE CAPTURE OF MONTAUBAN – 1st JULY 1916.

Montauban

7.30 a.m.

GERMANS

- - - GERMAN TRENCH SYSTEM (SIMPLIFIED)

BRITISH

18 KING'S L'POOL (2 L'POOL PALS)
19 M'CHESTERS (4 M'CHESTER PALS)
16 MANCHESTERS (1 M'CHESTER PALS)
17 MANCHESTERS (2 M'CHESTER PALS)
20 KING'S L'POOL (4 L'POOL PALS)
17 KING'S L'POOL (1 L'POOL PALS)

⎯⎯ BRITISH TRENCHES

Montauban

10.30 a.m.

GERMANS

- - - CAPTURED GERMAN TRENCH SYSTEM

16 MANCHESTERS (1 M'CHESTER PALS)
17 MANCHESTERS (2 M'CHESTER PALS)

BRITISH

FORMER BRITISH FRONT LINE

Two battalions of the Manchester Regiment lay down in the open until the machine-gun nest had been dealt with while all the time the British artillery plastered Montauban. At ten o'clock the artillery barrage lifted and the Manchesters swept forward in two waves to capture the devastated village, as thousands of demoralised Germans streamed northwards towards their rear positions. 30 Division had won a complete victory.

18 Division
Another New Army division, it was their first battle for the enthusiastic volunteers from the Home Counties and East Anglia.

Brigade	Battalion	Type	Origin
53rd	8/ Norfolk	New Army	Norwich
	6/ Royal Berkshire	New Army	Reading
	10/Essex	New Army	Warley
	8/Suffolk	New Army	Bury St. Edmunds
54th.	11/Royal Fusiliers	New Army	Hounslow
	7/Bedford	New Army	Bedford
	6/Northampton	New Army	Northampton
	12/Middlesex	New Army	Middlesex
55th.	7/Queen's	New Army	Guildford
	7/Buffs	New Army	Canterbury
	8/East Surrey	New Army	Kingston
	7/Royal West Kent	New Army	Maidstone
Pioneers	8/Royal Sussex	New Army	Chichester

Two mines were exploded prematurely, warning the Germans of the assault's exact time and when it began British losses were heavy. However, 30 Division's gains threatened the German line of retreat and as the defenders fell back the attackers, although with further heavy losses, pressed onwards until by noon 18 Division too had won all its objectives. The compete success of the XIII Corps had been brought about at a terrible price with over six thousand casualties.

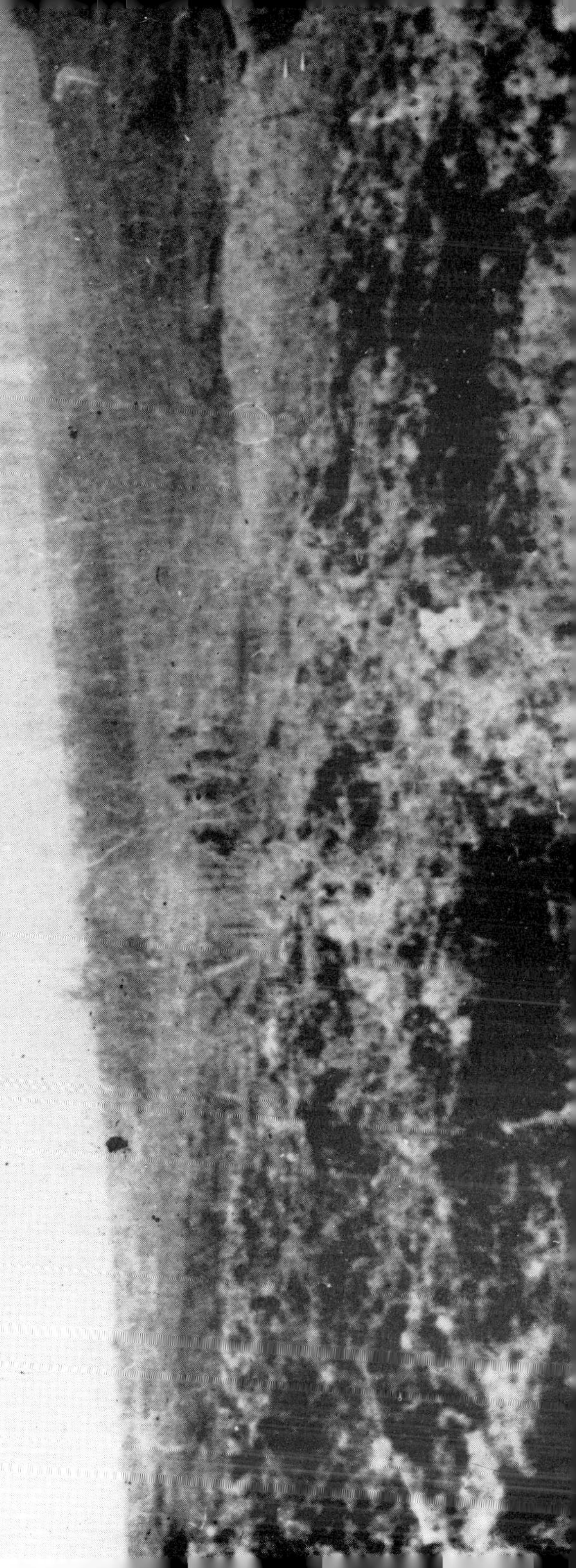

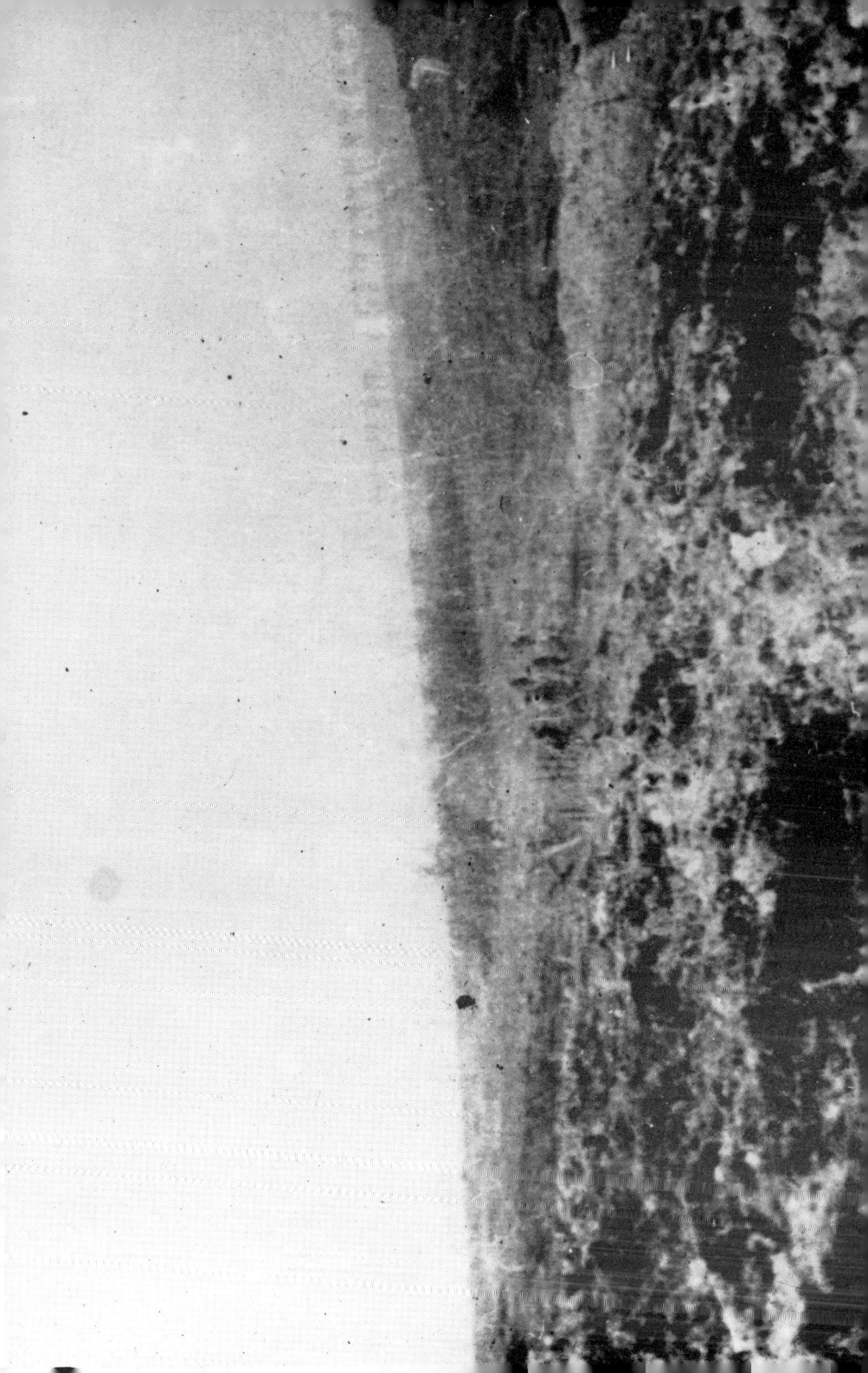

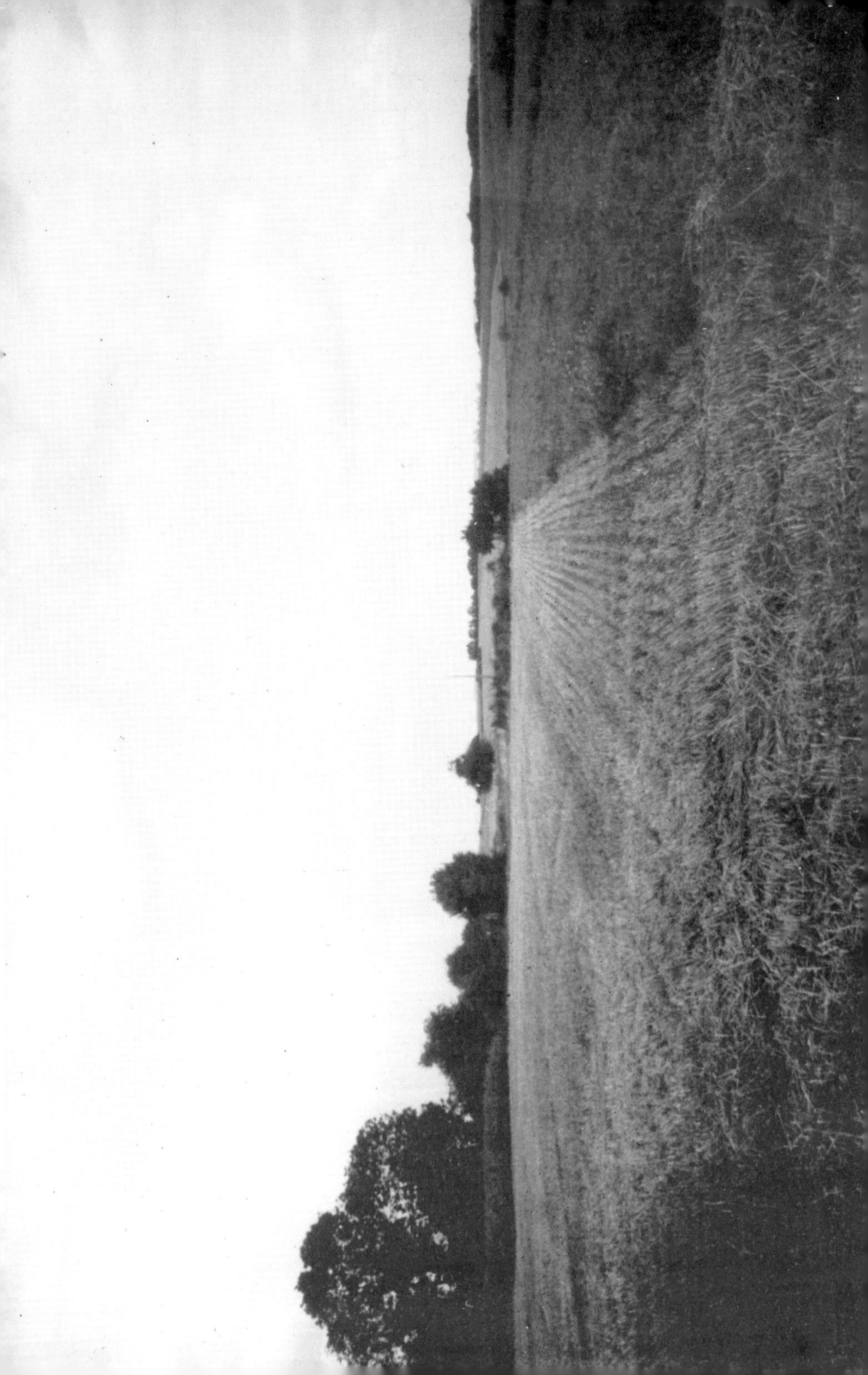

	CASUALTIES			
	Killed	Wounded	Missing	Total
30 Division officers	36	76	0	112
other ranks	792	2042	65	2899
18 Division officers	40	70	0	110
other ranks	872	2087	46	3015
Total	1170	4275	111	6136

The question must be asked, why was the XIII Corps' success not exploited? The French on their right had achieved equally brilliant results and were prepared to go on, as were the men of the 30 Division, despite their losses. 9 Division plus other troops were available in reserve. Failure on other parts of the battlefield led to XIII Corps being told to dig in where they were. The British Army had broken one of the most fundamental axioms of war, always reinforce success.

XV CORPS.

XV Corps was only partially successful. It faced German defences of exceptional strength, a maze of trenches 1,200 yards deep with fortified villages and numerous strong points, dug-outs and machine-gun nests. The plan was to by-pass Fricourt and Mametz then deal with them at leisure when the trench system was taken.

7 Division

This was another mixed unit of regulars and Kitchener volunteers with many of them drawn from the Manchester region.

Brigade	Battalion	Type	Origin
20th.	8/ Devonshire	New Army	Exeter
	9/Devonshire	New Army	Exeter
	2/Border	Regulars	
	2/Gordon Highlanders	Regulars	
22nd.	20/Manchester	New Army	5/Manchester Pals
	2/ Warwickshire	Regulars	
	1/Royal Welsh Fusiliers	Regulars	
	2/Royal Irish	Regulars	
91st.	21/Manchester	New Army	6/Manchester Pals
	22/Manchester	New Army	7/Manchester Pals
	2/Queens	Regulars	
	1/South Staffs	Regulars	
Pioneers	24/Manchester	New Army	Oldham Pals

On the right, 91st. Brigade's leading battalions, the 7th. Manchester Pals and the South Staffordshire regulars, reached the German trenches with few losses but when pushing onwards, suffered heavy casualties, especially from machine-guns. Helped by the successful advance of the XIII Corps on their right, which caused the Germans to fall back for fear of being surrounded, 91st. Brigade captured the second line of enemy trenches. The distance across No-Man's-Land had been only one to two hundred yards but machine guns had inflicted heavy casualties as the extended line advanced in the open. Private Whitworth of the Manchester Pals from Market Street, Tyldesley was a lucky survivor:-

> 'God only knows how I came out of it alive for I was knocked down by a shell. A piece of it struck my equipment and cut a strap but did not penetrate my body. I don't know how long I was on the ground but when I came round I saw dead and wounded lying all around me. I was lying under shell fire from eight in the morning until seven at night. I hope I shall never have to go through that ordeal again."
> L.J. 24th. July, 1916.

In the centre, 20th. Brigade had to advance over five hundred yards of cratered ground full of Germans. Despite casualties from machine-gun fire which broke the lines into small groups they reached the German defended area and began bombing and bayoneting the defenders. The 2/Border Regiment reached its objective but support failed to arrive. Without a supporting barrage, 20/Manchester and 1/Royal Welch Fusiliers which had been held in reserve, were sent forward to help and they too suffered heavy casualties.

21 Divison
With only three regular battalions this was almost entirely a New Army unit drawn mainly from the North East.

Brigade	Battalion	Type	Origin
62nd.	12/Northumberland Fusiliers	New Army	Newcastle
	13/Northumberland Fusiliers	New Army	Newcastle
	1/Lincoln	Regulars	
	10/Green Howards	New Army	Richmond

21 Divison cont.

Brigade	Battalion	Type	Origin
63rd.	8/Lincoln	New Army	Lincoln
	8/Somerset Light Infantry	New Army	Taunton
	4/Middlesex	Regulars	
	10/York & Lancaster	New Army	Pontefract
64th.	9/K.O.Y.L.I.	New Army	Pontefract
	10/K.O.Y.L.I.	New Army	Pontefract
	15/Durham Light Infantry	New Army	Newcastle
	1/East Yorkshire	Regulars	
Pioneers	14/Northumberland Fusiliers	New Army	Newcastle

On the left, the German front trenches were taken but with heavy losses and with no support on either flank it was all that they could do to hang on in the captured trenches against determined counter-attacks. In the centre and on the right, wave after wave of attackers were cut down by the German machine-guns which had been untouched by the artillery bombardment. In the afternoon a second frontal attack at Fricourt also failed with similar casualties, The unluckiest brigade on that day was the 50th., loaned from 17 Division in reserve. Attacking the strongest part of the Fricourt defences, wire intact, Germans ready, they came under murderous machine-gun and rifle fire. Whole lines fell in the first fifty yards and the attack was stopped in its tracks. The survivors lay out in shell holes until dark when they returned to the British lines.

17 Division.

Another division of New Army volunteers drawn mainly from the Midlands and the North of England, it was their first taste of action for the former civilians.

Brigade	Battalion	Type	Origin
50th.	10/West Yorkshire	New Army	York
	7/East Yorkshire	New Army	Beverley
	7/Green Howards	New Army	Richmond
	6/Dorsetshire	New Army	Dorchester
51st.	7/Lincolnshire	New Army	Lincoln
	7/Border	New Army	Carlisle
	8/South Staffordshire	New Army	Lichfield
	10/Sherwood Foresters	New Army	Derby

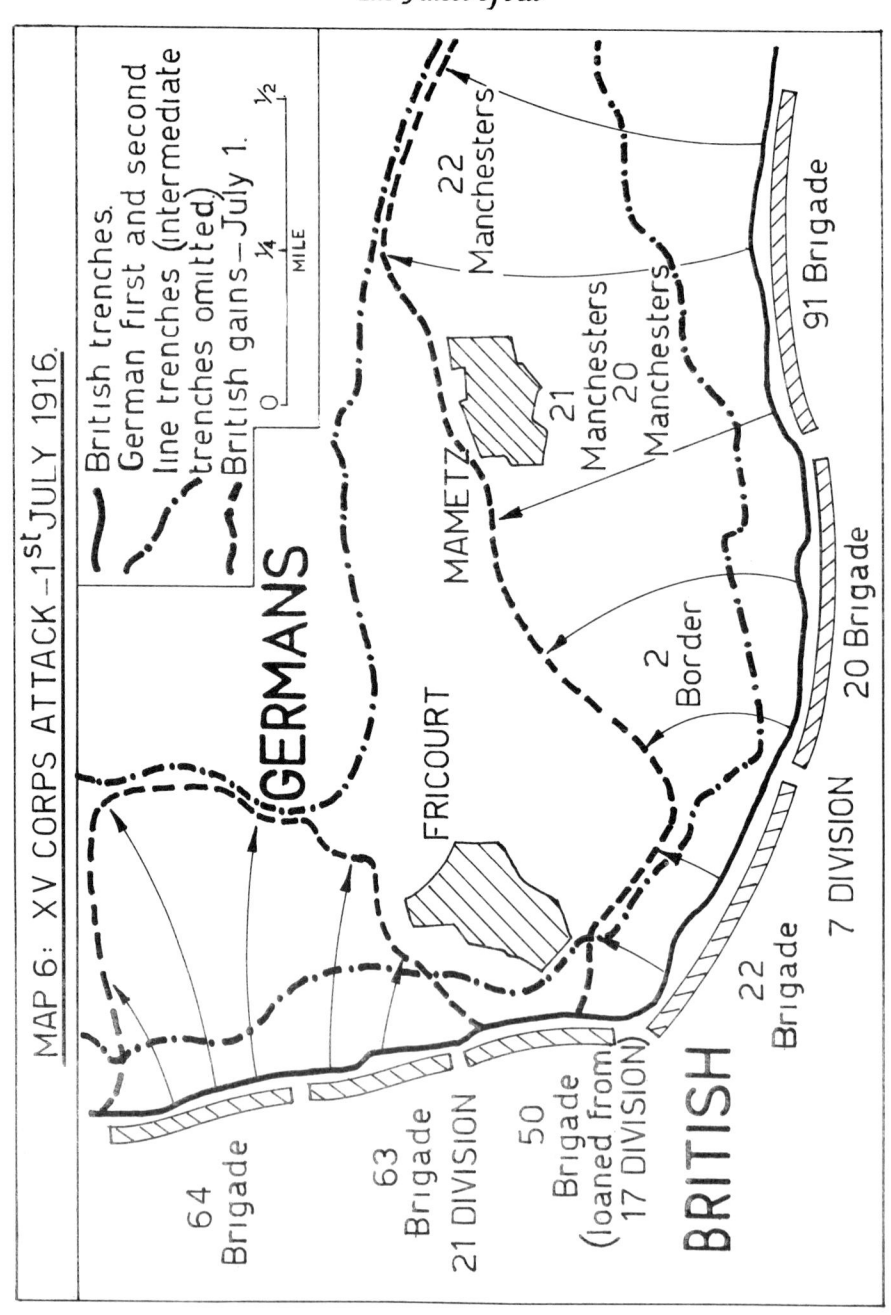

MAP 6: XV CORPS ATTACK – 1st JULY 1916.

17 Division cont.

Brigade	Battalion	Type	Origin
52nd.	9/Northumberland Fusiliers	New Army	Newcastle
	10/Lancashire Fusiliers	New Army	Bury
	9/Duke of Wellington	New Army	Halifax
	12/Manchester	New Army	Ashton-under-Lyne
Pioneers	7/York & Lancaster	New Army	Pontefract

Originally intended to be in Corps Reserve and to be used to exploit any breakthrough, 17 Division was held back, except for the 50th. Brigade which supported the attack. The remainder had the remarkable good luck to miss the holocaust of the 1st. July, 1916 and the lives of many local men were spared. Their turn was to come.

Although XV Corps had reached the German second line of trenches and had even captured Mametz village, the planned encirclement had failed, For this limited success the Corps had suffered losses of over eight thousand, due almost entirely to machine-gun fire:-

	CASUALTIES			
	Killed	Wounded	Missing	Total
7 Division officers	67	69	0	136
other ranks	965	2252	27	3244
18 Division officers	91	103	1	195
other ranks	1091	2859	111	4061
17 Division officers	21	21	0	42
(50 Brigade) other ranks	536	544	33	1113
Total	2771	5848	172	8791

III CORPS

III Corps had to attack one of the most carefully constructed defensive networks of the entire front, It was a formidable, if not impossible task.

34 Division

This was another volunteer division, drawn mainly from the North East of England.

Brigade	Battalion	Type	Origin
101st.	15/Royal Scots Fusiliers	New Army	1/Edinburgh Pals
	16/Royal Scots Fusiliers	New Army	2/Edinburgh Pals
	10/Lincolnshire	New Army	Grimsby Chums
	11/Suffolk	New Army	Cambridge
102nd.	20/Northumberland Fusiliers	New Army	1/Tyneside Scots
	21/Northumberland Fusiliers	New Army	2/Tyneside Scots
	22/Northumberland Fusiliers	New Army	3/Tyneside Scots
	23/Northumberland Fusiliers	New Army	4/Tyneside Scots
103rd.	24/Northumberland Fusiliers	New Army	1/Tyneside Irish
	25/Northumberland Fusiliers	New Army	2/Tyneside Irish
	26/Northumberland Fusiliers	New Army	3/Tyneside Irish
	27/Northumberland Fusiliers	New Army	4/Tyneside Irish
Pioneers	18/Northumberland Fusiliers	New Army	1/Tyneside Pioneers

Two of the attacking brigades came from a region where the response to Kitchener's call for volunteers had been more than enthusiastic. One county regiment, the Northumberland Fusiliers, was able to raise thirty service battalions for the New Army. As a recruitment ploy several battalions had formed as 'Tyneside Irish' or 'Tyneside Scottish' although the Celtic connections of most recruits was somewhat tenuous. Those volunteering for the Irish were attracted by the pugnacious reputation of the regular Irish regiments while those joining the Scottish were influenced by the possibility of wearing a kilt! In the event the nearest they got to wearing tartan was a square of tartan material behind their cap badge.

The assault was on a narrow frontage, barely four hundred yards wide, in four columns each of four battalions deep, a formation which invited confusion and slaughter, indeed within ten minutes of the attack, some eighty per cent of the leading battalions were casualties. On the right, the German front trenches were overrun but the attackers were checked there, in the centre most of the attackers were pinned down in No-Man's-Land, while on the left the advance was driven back to the British trenches.

8 Division

Originally a division of the old regular army, 8 Division had fought in France since 1914, losing heavily, and had exchanged one veteran brigade for one of Kitchener's volunteers.

Brigade	Battalion	Type	Origin
23rd.	2/Devonshire	Regulars	
	2/West Yorkshire	Regulars	
	2/Middlesex	Regulars	
	2/Scottish Rifles	Regulars	
25th.	2/Lincolnshire	Regulars	
	2/Berkshire	Regulars	
	1/Royal Irish Rifles	Regulars	
	2/Rifle Brigade	Regulars	
70th.	11/Sherwood Foresters	New Army	Derby
	8/K.OY.L.I.	New Army	Pontefract
	8/York & Lancaster	New Army	Pontefract
	9/York & Lancaster	New Army	Pontefract
Pioneers	22/Durham L.I.	New Army	Durham

In this sector, the artillery barrage proved useless. The Germans were ready from the start and machine-gun fire played havoc with the advancing lines. Miraculously some men reached the German trenches but determined counter-attacks drove them out again.

Private Thomas Clegg was one of those hit. A miner, he had gone to find work in the expanding Yorkshire coalfield and had enlisted with his new chums. A friend wrote to his widow in Plank Lane, Leigh:-

> "Nobly, bravely and willingly doing his duty that morning he marched into the hellish fire of our enemies with such cool and undaunting spirit that no wonder words of praise were showered on them all."
> L.J. 28th. July, 1916.

Two coalminers and neighbours in Samuel Street, Hindsford, who had joined up together in the same regiment, the 9/York and Lancaster, were brought down by shrapnel at the same time. Signaller William

Hankinson, a single man aged 25 years was hit in both legs and forced to crawl five hundred yards back to his own trenches, accompanied by his friend, Private Edward Haseldene, wounded in the shoulder at the same time.

19 Division

Yet another volunteer division, this one came form the western counties of England so contained scores of local men.

Brigade	Battalion	Type	Origin
56th.	7/King's Own	New Army	Lancaster
	7/East Lancashire	New Army	Preston
	7/South Lancashire	New Army	Warrington
	7/Loyal North Lancashire	New Army	Preston
57th.	10/Warwickshire	New Army	Warwick
	8/Gloucestershire	New Army	Bristol
	10/Worcestershire	New Army	Worcester
	8/North Staffordshire	New Army	Lichfield
58th.	9/Cheshire	New Army	Chester
	9/Royal Welch Fusiliers	New Army	Wrexham
	9/Welch	New Army	Cardiff
	6/Wiltshire	New Army	Devizes
Pioneers	5/South Wales Borderers	New Army	Brecon

All day, 19 Division waited in reserve and watched the dust of battle in front and the steady stream of wounded men coming back past them. As the attack collapsed, 19 Division was ordered to attack at 5 p.m. that evening. Then occurred one of the few incidents of good fortune for local men in the entire war. At 4.15 p.m., as the battalions were marching grimly into their assembly positions, the order was cancelled and 19 Division returned to its bivouacs, like 17 Division, the luckiest men in the army

Their turn was yet to come, but the attack had completely failed. III Corps suffered the heaviest casualties of the two-division Corps engaged on the opening day, over eleven thousand men, but had nothing to show for its losses except two tiny, pathetic footholds in the enemy's front trenches.

	CASUALTIES			
	Killed	**Wounded**	**Missing**	**Total**
7 Division officers	67	69	0	136
other ranks	965	2252	27	3244
8 Division officers	99	92	9	200
other ranks	1828	3003	90	4921
34 Division officers	113	148	4	256
other ranks	2367	3439	309	6115
Total	4407	6682	412	11501

In the twenty four hours following 6 a.m. on the 1st. July, the III Corps field ambulances evacuated 4,993 wounded from No-Man's-Land and so great were the numbers that it was not until 3rd. July, that the last man was brought in by the tireless devoted stretcher bearers.

X CORPS

X Corps was given the task of capturing the western edge of the Thiepval Plateau which would have opened up the entire German position. The impressive natural defences had been further improved, and worse still, the artillery barrage again proved ineffective. Once the attacking infantry showed themselves the German machine guns immediately opened up.

32 Division

32 Division was anther unit of volunteers stiffened with regular battalions and containing many local men.

Brigade	**Battalion**	**Type**	**Origin**
14th.	19/ Lancashire Fusiliers	New Army	3/Salford Pals
	1/Dorset	Regulars	
	2/Manchester	Regulars	
	15/Highland L.I.	New Army	Glasgow Tramways
96th.	15/Lancashire Fusiliers	New Army	1/Salford Pals
	16/Lancashire Fusiliers	New Army	2/Salford Pals
	16/Northumberland Fusiliers	New Army	Newcastle Commercials
	2/Royal Iniskilling Fusiliers	Regulars	

32 Division cont.

Brigade	Battalion	Type	Origin
97th.	16/ Highland L.I.	New Army	Glasgow Boy's Brigade
	17/ Highland L.I.	New Army	Glasgow Commercials
	11/Border	New Army	Lonsdales
	2/K.O.Y.L.I.	Regulars	
Pioneers	17/Northumberland Fusiliers	New Army	Railway Pals

The commander of the 97th. Brigade had been an observer in the Russo-Japanese War of 1904-05, where he had noticed that before an attack, the Japanese infantry crept as close as possible to where their artillery barrage was falling, so he sent his men out into No-Man's-Land before the British bombardment stopped in order to shorten the length of time during which they would be exposed to the enemy's fire. Private Tom Hector of the Border Regiment thoroughly approved of the tactic:-

"They placed their shells perfectly, a chalk line with us twenty five yards behind. Then they raised their fire[1] and we got at Fritz with the bayonet."
W.E. 14th. Oct., 1916.

It was of no avail. Once the British infantry showed themselves the German machine-guns opened up as if there had been no bombardment. Despite this, and the heavy losses it caused the brigade captured the front line trenches.

The 96th. Brigade fared no better. Following a football drop-kicked into No-Man's-Land, they hurled themselves forward only for the lines of men to be swept away by the intense fire. Even so about a hundred of the 15/Lancashire Fusiliers (1st. Salford Pals) reached the enemy trenches but instead of eliminating the defenders skulking in the deep dug-outs, they impulsively rushed on so that the Germans emerged behind them and mowed down the supporting waves. The Salford men kept going and linked up with the Irish on their left while the enemy re-occupied their trenches behind them.

[1] Aimed their shells 100 yards further on.

36 (Ulster) Division
Recruited mainly from among the fiercely patriotic Protestants of the Irish province of Ulster, this unique division advanced with religious fervour.

Brigade	Battalion	Type	Origin
107th.	8/Royal Irish Rifles	New Army	Belfast
	9/Royal Irish Rifles	New Army	Belfast
	10/Royal Irish Rifles	New Army	Belfast
	13/Royal Irish Rifles	New Army	Belfast
108th.	11/Royal Irish Rifles	New Army	Antrim
	12/Royal Irish Rifles	New Army	Antrim
	13/Royal Irish Rifles	New Army	Down
	19 Royal Irish Fusiliers	New Army	Armagh, Cavan & Monaghan
109th.	9/Royal Inniskilling Fusiliers	New Army	Tyrone
	10/Royal Inniskilling Fusiliers	New Army	Derry
	14/Royal Irish Rifles	New Army	Belfast
	11/Royal Inniskilling Fusiliers	New Army	Donegal & Fermanagh
Pioneers	16/Royal Irish Rifles	New Army	Down

Although the advance on the left failed to make progress against defenders who were ready for them, on the right the German defences were successfully carried and the Ulstermen rushed impetuously onwards, capturing the formidable Schwaben Redoubt and even reaching the top of the Thiepval Plateau. They hung on all day in shell holes and captured German trenches, counter-attacked on three sides, as casualties grew and ammunition diminished until at ten o'clock in the evening they withdrew to the old German front line trenches. Even among this division there were local men, who because of their Irish ancestry, had volunteered for Irish Regiments. Here too there were local casualties[1]. Among the Irish officers killed were E. Hewitt and W.A. Hewitt, both brothers of the Reverend Hewitt, Vicar of St. Mark's, Haydock. Their other brother had been killed at Festubert in 1915.

[1] See Appendix

49 Division

This territorial division had already seen action around Ypres in December, 1915 when it suffered almost a thousand casualties during a German gas attack.

Brigade	Battalion	Type	Origin
146th.	1/5West Yorkshire	Territorial	York
	1/6West Yorkshire	Territorial	Bradford
	1/7West Yorkshire	Territorial	Leeds
	1/8West Yorkshire	Territorial	Leeds
147th.	1/4Duke of Wellington	Territorial	Halifax
	1/5Duke of Wellington	Territorial	Huddersfield
	1/6Duke of Wellington	Territorial	Skipton
	1/7Duke of Wellington	Territorial	Milnsbridge
148th.	1/4York & Lancaster Fusiliers	Territorial	Sheffield
	1/5York & Lancaster Fusiliers	Territorial	Rotherham
	1/4K.O.Y.L.I.	Territorial	Wakefield
	1/5K.O.Y.L.I.	Territorial	Doncaster
Pioneers	1/3Monmouth	Territorial	Aberganenny

49 Division had been held in reserve, earmarked to exploit gaps made in the German line by 32 and 36 Divisions. As early as 8.30 a.m., it was warned to be ready but its planned pursuit of a beaten, fleeing enemy was not to be. Instead it was used piecemeal to prop up the flagging attacks of the other two divisions, All day it battled to protect the flanks of the Ulstermen trapped in the Schwaben Redoubt. X Corps attack had completely failed with immense losses. Total casualties of the three divisions were over nine thousand, more than half of them in the Ulster Division.

	CASUALTIES			
	Killed	**Wounded**	**Missing**	**Total**
32 Division officers	53	99	6	158
other ranks	1230	2453	108	3791
36 Division officers	79	102	8	189
other ranks	1777	2626	370	4773
49 Division officers	5	41	0	46
other ranks	126	412	6	544
Total	3280	5733	498	9501

VIII CORPS
VIII Corps attacked the most formidable German defences along the entire Somme position. Carefully constructed earthworks added strength to the natural features, the entire section dominated by the fortified village of Beaumont Hamel.

29 Division.
During 1915 this regular division had endured the hell of the Dardenelles campaign[1] and in March, 1916, it was transferred to France just in time to be plunged into the holocaust of the Somme.

Brigade	Battalion	Type	Origin
86th.	1/Lancashire Fusiliers	Regulars	
	2/Royal Fusiliers	Regulars	
	1/Royal Dublin Fusiliers	Regulars	
	16/Middlesex	New Army	Public Schools Battalion
87th.	2.South Wales Borders	Regulars	
	1/K.S.O.B.	Regulars	
	1/Royal Inniskilling	Regulars	
	1/Border	Regulars	
88th.	1/Essex	Regulars	
	Newfoundland	New Army	Canada
	2/Hampshire	Regulars	
	4/Worcester	Regulars	
Pioneers	1/2Monmouth	Territorial	Pontypool

Ten minutes before zero hour, a huge mine, the Hawthorn Mine, was exploded beneath the German trenches which, although it inflicted heavy casualties, warned the defenders that an attack was imminent. The frontal attack on the heavily fortified village of Beaumont Hamel was led by the 1/Lancashire Fusiliers who made for a sunken road halfway across No-Man's-Land:-

> "The leading two lines, B and D companies were practically wiped out within a few yards of the sunken road and only some wounded managed to crawl back. Captain Dawson and Company

---
[1] See companion volume, 'Just Like Hell, Local Men at Gallipoli,'

The Finest of All

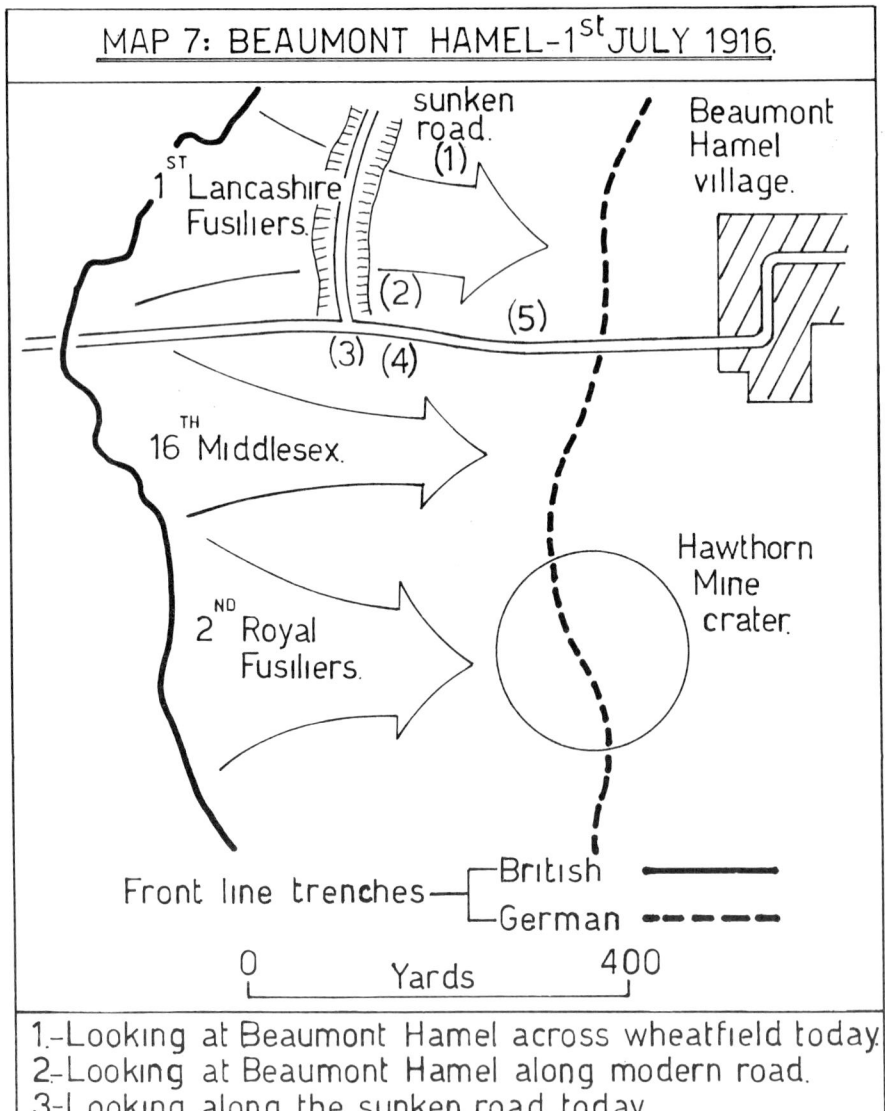

MAP 7: BEAUMONT HAMEL – 1st JULY 1916.

- sunken road. (1)
- 1ST Lancashire Fusiliers
- Beaumont Hamel village.
- (2)
- (3) (4) (5)
- 16TH Middlesex.
- Hawthorn Mine crater.
- 2ND Royal Fusiliers.

Front line trenches — British ——
                     German - - - -

0   Yards   400

1.- Looking at Beaumont Hamel across wheatfield today.
2.- Looking at Beaumont Hamel along modern road.
3.- Looking along the sunken road today.
4.- Looking at Hawthorn Mine crater today.
5.- British and German (unexploded) trench mortars found here.

The Finest of All

Sergeant Major Nelson were hit as they stood on the parapet giving the order to advance."
War Diary, 1/LF, PRO. 95. 2300.

The survivors darted from shell hole to shell hole until only a few small, isolated parties were left and finally they were halted well short of the German positions. Scores of local men were among the casualties in this popular regiment. Private Tom Hilton, of 11, Leigh Street, Leigh, was wounded as was Private Edgar Green of 161, Chapel Street, Leigh who, before the war, worked at Alder Mills, hit in the left arm. Private Walter White of 15, Wilson Street, Leigh, was hit in the right shoulder and side by shrapnel but much worse, Private David Taylor of Samuel Street, Hindsford, a moulder at the local iron foundry, lost an arm, blown off by a shellburst. Private Fred Lowe from Astley, a bank clerk at Parr's Bank, Leigh, went down wounded as the men rushed forward at the German trenches.

No-Man's-Land was littered with the bodies of the dead and wounded, the paths through the wire were so choked that the supporting waves could not get through and the communication trenches became clogged as injured men made their way to the rear. Among them were Private Jack Houghton of Trafalgar Street, Leigh, Private Ralph Ackers of Thirlemere Street, Leigh, Private William Hilton of Strange Street, Leigh, Private Porter from Glazebury, Private Disley from Clifton Street, Leigh and Private William Henry Bandy from Howe Bridge. Private Sidlow of Elliot Street, Tyldesley, hit by shrapnel in the back, lay out in the open for three days before being brought in and Private Harman from Leigh was buried by a shellburst and dug out wounded but alive.

The list of local wounded seemed endless. Two more Tyldesley men in the Lancashire Fusiliers became casualties, Private Speakman, a veteran of the Dardenelles campaign, from Factory Street, was hit in both shoulders while Private Alfred Jackson of Bank Street, another Dardenelles veteran, was brought down by shrapnel striking his right thigh. Lance-Corporal James Brown, of Selwyn Street, Leigh, fifteen years a regular, was shot in the ankle in addition to being hit by shrapnel in the right arm. Some survivors took shelter in the sunken road where they could neither advance nor retreat.

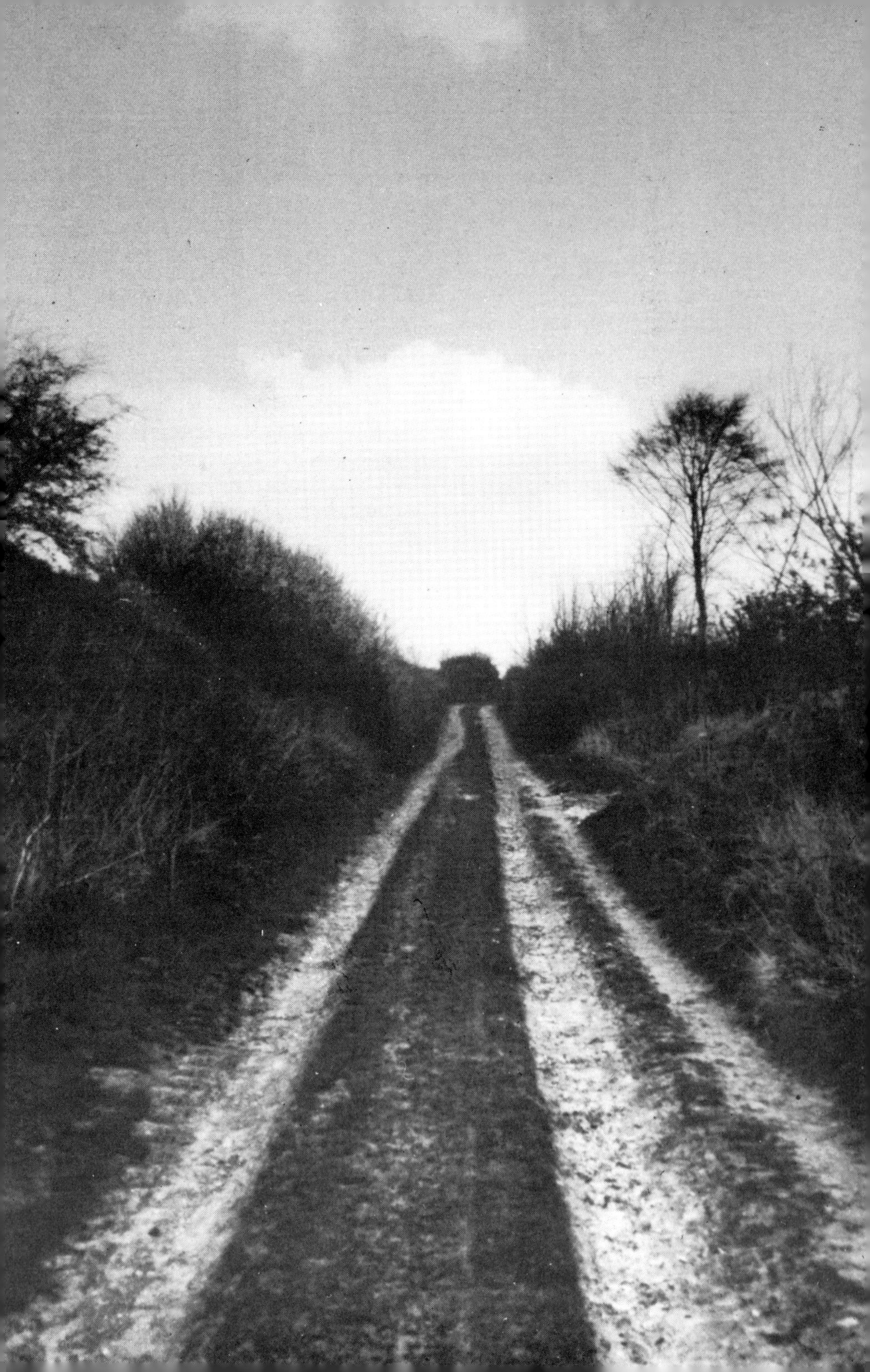

The Finest of All

The Lancashire men rushed forward through the hail of machine-gun bullets and the explosion of the artillery shells and were brought down in droves, particularly in the Border Regiment. Lance-Corporal Herbert Martland was hit in the hand by a bullet, Private William Stewart was hit in the arm by shrapnel, Private John Wesley had his foot blown off by a shell. Private John Gornall was also wounded in the leg by a shell but the surgeons managed to save it. Another local officer, Lieutenant J.B. Sinclair, 22 years old and an old boy of Upholland Grammar School, won the Military Cross serving with the Border Regiment as he courageously led his men by example through fire and smoke. One of the wounded, Private Disley, wrote of his experiences:-

> "I went out over the top in a bombing party of eleven men. There is only me and the Sergeant left. He is wounded and I have lost an arm and a leg. Private Harris from Tyldesley was with me. I was just throwing a bomb when my officer was hit in the head. I picked him up and was just dragging him to safety when a shell hit both of us. When I recovered I dragged myself to the trenches where the stretcher bearers were and was sent to the hospital the day following."
> L.J. 28th. July, 1916.

Major Utterson and forty men of the Lancashire Fusiliers left the British trenches about noon to reinforce their comrades pinned down in the sunken road. Only the Major and three men reached them. With all company commanders gone, Lieutenant Colonel Magniac, the Fusiliers' Battalion C.O., went forward to the sunken road himself and attempted to direct operations., Private John Livesley from Higher Ince, actually reached the German trench with a bombing party and was pulled over the parapet by the defenders, never to be seen again by his comrades, his death being confirmed only months later in exchange of lists between the two sides.

4 Division

One of the very few all-regular divisions, this unit was a veteran of many earlier battles in France.

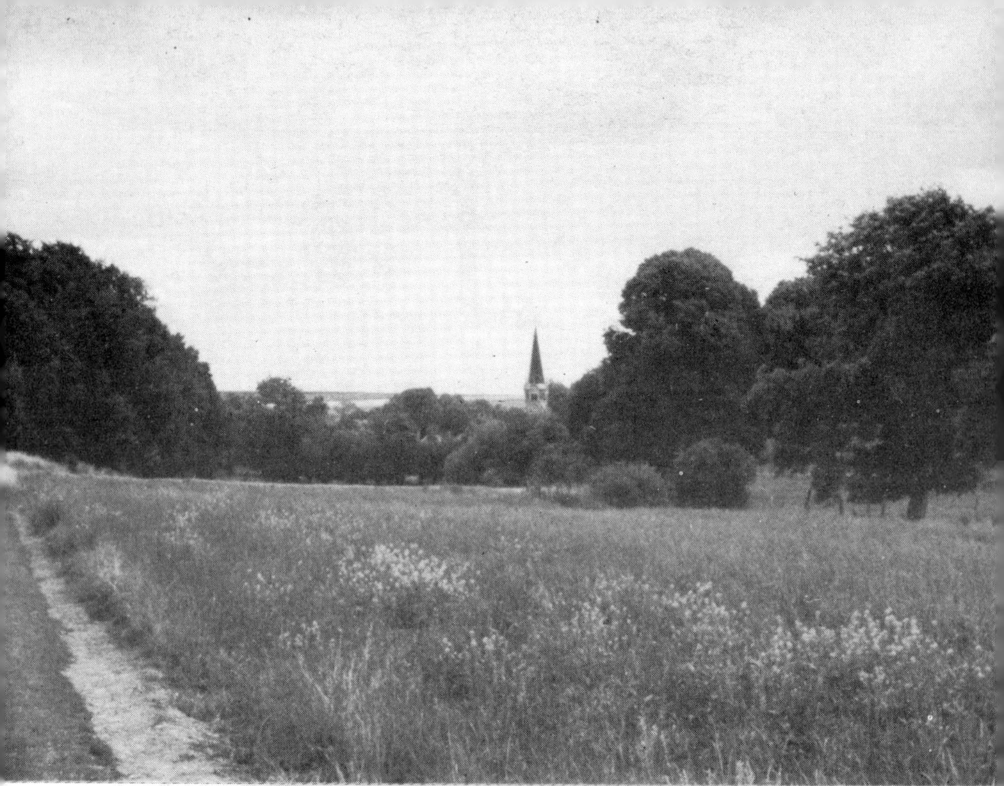

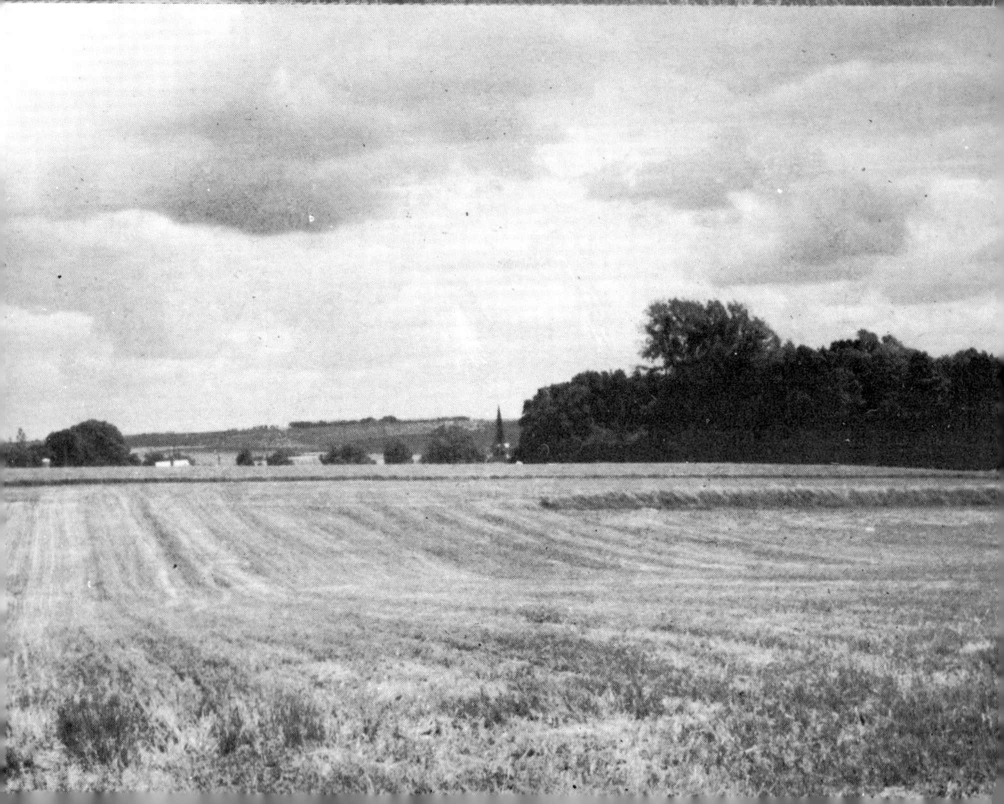

Brigade	Battalion	Type	Origin
10th.	1/Royal Irish Fusiliers	Regular	
	2/Royal Dublin Fusiliers	Regular	
	2/Seaforth Highlanders	Regular	
	1/Warwickshire	Reguar	
11th.	1/Somerset Light Infantry	Regular	
	1/East Lancashire	Regular	
	1/Hampshire	Regular	
	1/Rifle Brigade	Regular	
88th.	1/King's Own	Regular	
	2/Lancashire Fusiliers	Regular	
	2/Duke of Wellington's	Regular	
	2/Essex	Regular	
Pioneers	2/West Yorkshire	New Army	Leeds

Although the wire was well cut by the artillery, four German machine-guns survived and shot down all the leading battalions, slaughtered the supports and prevented reinforcements and supplies from reaching the few survivors who had reached the German front trenches. Supporting Brigades, including 2/Lancashire Fusiliers, were ordered forward and although the order was cancelled, it came too late to prevent further losses. Private Jacob Fielding of 277, Leigh Road, Leigh was shot in the knee and found himself in the field hospital next to Private Tom Griffiths, another Leigh man in the 2/Lancashire Fusiliers who had also been wounded.

31 Division

Another division of Kitchener's volunteers from the North of England, it had been sent to Egypt in December, 1915 but recalled and diverted to France when the Gallipoli Campaign collapsed. This was its first action.

Brigade	Battalion	Type	Origin
92nd.	10/East Yorkshire	New Army	Hull Commercials
	11/East Yorkshire	New Army	Hull Tradesmen
	12/East Yorkshire	New Army	Hull Sportsmen
	13/East Yorkshire	New Army	T'Others
93rd.	15/West Yorkshire	New Army	Leeds Pals
	16/West Yorkshire	New Army	1/Bradford Pals
	18/West Yorkshire	New Army	2/Bradford Pals
	18/Durham Light Infantry	New Army	Durham Pals

31 Division cont.

Brigade	Battalion	Type	Origin
94th.	11/East Lancashire	New Army	Accrington Pals
	12/York & Lancaster	New Army	Sheffield Pals
	13/York & Lancaster	New Army	1/Barnsley Pals
	14/York & Lancaster	New Army	2/Barnsley Pals
Pioneers	12/K.O.Y.L.I.	New Army	Halifax Pals

Twelve Pals' Battalions went over the top including the famous Accrington Pals, in an attack which exemplifies the poignant destiny of these volunteer soldiers. Once more the Germans were waiting. The British Official History graphically describes the Pals' progress across No-Man's-Land:-

> "The extended lines started in excellent order but gradually melted away. There was no wavering or attempting to go back, the men fell in their ranks before the first hundred yards had been crossed. The magnificent gallantry, discipline and determination displayed by all ranks of this North Country division were of no avail against the concentrated fire of the enemy's infantry and artillery."

Only a few isolated parties reached the German trenches where most of them were pinned down, unable to advance further.

> "Small parties penetrated as far as the German fourth line trench but were never seen again.'
> War Diary, 11/East Lancs. WO 95. 2339.

Some parties were not so small. At about 8.30 a.m., one hundred men of the 11/East Lancashire Regiment (Accrington Pals) entered Serre village, which at that time the Germans were shelling and were wiped out. Not only the riflemen suffered heavy casualties. Of the nine machine-gun teams which went forward with the 92nd. Brigade (four officers and 63 men) two thirds of the force became casualties, five killed, twenty wounded and eighteen missing.

48 (South Midlands) Division

These were territorial soldiers who had volunteered to serve overseas and for the most of them it was their first action.

Brigade	Battalion	Type	Origin
143rd.	1/5Warwickshire	Territorial	Birmingham
	1/6Warwickshire	Territorial	Birmingham
	1/7Warwickshire	Territorial	Coventry
	1/8Warwickshire	Territorial	Birmingham
144th.	1/4Gloucestershire	Territorial	Bristol
	1/6Gloucestershire	Territorial	Bristol
	1/7Worcestershire	Territorial	Kidderminster
	1/8Worcestershire	Territorial	Worcester
145th.	1/5Gloucestershire	Territorial	Gloucester
	1/4Oxford & Bucks	Territorial	Oxford
	1/4Berkshire	Territorial	Reading
	1/1Buckinghamshire	Territorial	Aylesbury
Pioneers	1/5Sussex	Territorial	Hastings

Fortunately for the division, half were stationed on the extreme left where no attack was planned while the other half were in reserve except for two battalions of the 143rd. Brigade who attacked with 4 Division. The remainder avoided the slaughter of 1st. July, 1916. J.W. 'Jock' Bamforth of Birch House in Upholland, in later life a well known and respected headmaster, had just completed his teacher training course at Saltley College, Birmingham when war broke out in 1914 and together with several fellow students he volunteered for the 1/8 Royal Warwickshire Regiment which was one of the two battalions detached to 4 Division. He was in the first wave to go over the top:-

> 'At 7.29 a.m., we were ordered to lie on the parapet and at exactly 7.30 a.m., we were given the order to advance. We had to advance at walking pace, rifles in the air (a new method). We had hardly got the order when every gun in Germany blazed away at us, especially machine-guns which did all the damage. Before we crossed No-Man's-Land we had lost practically half the Battalion. We reached the fourth German line and held it for about four hours when we had spent our stock of bombs and

ammunition and we were not able to communicate with our H.Q."
W.E. 13th. July, 1916.

Private Bamforth was one of a party of about seventy men who were almost cut off and were forced to fight their way back. Fortunately most succeeded but VIII Corps attack had failed completely.

VIII Corps suffered more casualties, over fourteen thousand, than any other Corps on 1st. July, 1916. The trenches were crowded with dead and wounded with many lying out in No-Man's-Land. From noon until four in the afternoon the British artillery was silent, and so the Germans allowed stretcher-bearers to bring in the wounded but when the British guns re-opened fire, the Germans returned fire preventing further movement until ten o'clock at night. From then until dawn the next day. ambulancemen, artillerymen, engineers and infantry toiled to bring in the wounded and it was not until 3rd. July that No-Man's-Land was reported clear.

	CASUALTIES			
	Killed	Wounded	Missing	Total
29 Division officers	106	111	7	224
other ranks	1489	2996	242	4727
4 Division[1] officers	136	134	876	346
other ranks	1842	3429	290	5561
31 Division officers	69	83	7	159
other ranks	1282	2116	75	3473
Total	4924	8869	697	14490

VII CORPS

To the north of the main attack, VII Corps of the Third Army, made a diversionary attack against Gommecourt with two divisions of territorial troops. The operation was to make the Germans believe that this was the real attack and German batteries opened up as early as 4 a.m. Of all the blunders perpetrated by British Army planners on the 1st. July, 1916, this was surely the most criminal. Diversionary attacks

---
[1]Including two Battalions of the 143rd. Brigade, 48th. (Midland) Division.

should be made against the enemy's weaker positions not his strongest. Worse still, not only was Gommecourt particularly easy to defend, the approach to it was so exposed that it was impossible to disengage from a failed attack without suffering extra losses. All this was perfectly well known to the British High Command. No German troops were diverted from further south and the diversion was an expensive failure.

56 (London) Division

These territorials had been in France since 1914, attached to regular divisions to strengthen them and were now, for the first time, assembled together in their own Division.

Brigade	Battalion	Type	Origin
167th.	1/1London Regiment	Territorial	Bloomsbury
	1/3London Regiment	Territorial	Hampstead
	1/7Middlesex	Territorial	Hornsea
	1/8Middlesex	Territorial	Hounslow
168th.	1/4London Regiment	Territorial	City Road
	1/12London Regiment	Territorial	Rangers
	1/13London Regiment	Territorial	Kensington
	1/14London Regiment	Territorial	London Scottish
169th.	1/2London Regiment	Territorial	Westminster
	1/3London Regiment	Territorial	London Rifles
	1/9London Regiment	Territorial	Queen Victoria's Rifles
	1/16London Regiment	Territorial	Westminster Rifles
Pioneers	1/5Cheshire Regiment	Territorial	Chester

A determined charge took the Londoners into the German defences but losses were enormous and even here one of them had a local connection[1].

46 (North Midland) Division

These territorials had to create a diversion and at the same time protect the left flank of the attack in a similar attack to the Londoners.

[1] See Major Francis Lindsay in Appendix.

Brigade	Battalion	Type	Origin
137th.	1/5 South Staffordshire	Territorial	Walsall
	1/6 South Staffordshire	Territorial	Wolverhampton
	1/5 North Staffordshire	Territorial	Hanley
	1/6 North Staffordshire	Territorial	Burton
138th.	1/4 Lincolnshire	Territorial	Lincoln
	1/5 Lincolnshire	Territorial	Grimsby
	1/4 Lincolnshire	Territorial	Leicester
	1/5 Lincolnshire	Territorial	Loughborough
139th.	1/5 Sherwod Foresters	Territorial	Derby
	1/6 Sherwod Foresters	Territorial	Chesterfield
	1/7 Sherwod Foresters	Territorial	Nottingham
	1/8 Sherwod Foresters	Territorial	Newark
Pioneers	1/1 Monmouthshire	Territorial	Newport

The division made a futile frontal attack on prepared German positions and only a handful of men reached the first line of trenches. In its vain attempt to 'divert against itself, forces which might otherwise be directed against the left flank of the main attack[1]'", VII Corps had lost nearly seven thousand casualties.

	CASUALTIES			
	Killed	Wounded	Missing	Total
46 Division officers	50	71	16	137
other ranks	803	1340	175	2318
56 Division officers	53	107	23	183
other ranks	1300	2248	583	4131
Total	2206	3766	797	6669

---

[1] Official orders.

CHAPTER V The Fight Goes On.

The battle did not end at dusk on the 1st. July, 1916. Although British G.H.Q. had no plans for a resumption of the offensive, several aggressive actions were initiated at Corps level and for a fortnight, from the 2nd. to the 13th, July, the British struggled forward, trying to establish themselves within assaulting position of the German second line of defence on the main ridge. Simultaneously, the Germans hastily repaired their battered defences and both sides brought in replacement troops. During the next four months, all British divisions in France, except two, were used in the Somme battles, some several times, so that almost every local man serving on the Western Front during 1916 took part in the Battle of the Somme. It is almost impossible to keep count of the local casualties, there were so many.

On 14th. July, the British attacked again in a more modest yet a more imaginative concept. In a night attack over 22,000 men of the XIII Corps and the XIV Corps assembled in No-Man's-Land and after only a five minute bombardment, rushed forward to capture a five mile length of front that on the 1st. July had been the German second line. Unfortunately yet again this initial success was not followed up and another chance for a breakthrough was lost. For two months until 31st. August, the British attacks continued. Slowly, yard by yard, more enemy territory was taken but at a terrible cost in lives. All through this bitter non-stop fighting the men were, as the Official History states:-

> 'subjected to heavy losses, great hardships and tremendous physical and moral strain, they had only their own dogged spirit to maintain them."

Private Wharf was blown up by a 'Jack Johnson' (a shell named after the American negro boxer with a big knock out punch) and buried so that it took an hour to dig him out. Writing home to his wife in Leigh, he summed up:-

> "The fighting here is indescribable. I am sure that Verdun is not in it."
> L.J. 14th. July, 1916.

Sergeant Fred Dale from Parbold agreed:-

> "The marvel to me is not how many get killed or wounded but how you come out alive at all, Words are too weak to describe the fighting on the Somme."
> W.E. 9th. Sept., 1916.

Not so lucky was Lance-Corporal Ben Lloyd, 7/South Lancashire Regiment of 36, Knowsley Road, Leigh, a drawer at Plank Lane Colliery who was also blown up by artillery. His friend, Levi Pemberton, was wounded by a fragment of the same shell and wrote home:-

> "We could not find him."
> L.C. 4th. August, 1916

Aged 30 years, Lloyd left a wife and three children. As the fighting continued, there were countless acts of heroism, few of which gained official recognition. However, one did, when Lance Corporal, Frank Turner, R.A.M.C. of 163, Bag Lane, Atherton, was awarded the D.C.M. As the battle raged over a shattered village Turner saw half a dozen wounded men lying in the street:-

> "There was a perfect storm of bullets and shrapnel., Down on my stomach I crawled inch by inch along that wrecked street. It seemed a terribly long way to the first man. The enemy at the other end of the street were waiting for any glimpse of life. It seemed hours before I reached the first poor chap and the real work began as I had to draw him back inch by inch. At last I reached shelter and beads of sweat dripped off my face."
> L.J. 20th. Oct., 1916.

Five times Turner went out and was wounded twice. He saved four men, the last man was killed by a sniper as he was being pulled along to safety.

In one attack on the seemingly impregnable Thiepval position, a platoon of the Lancashire Fusiliers lost all its men except one, Richard Green from Scot Lane, Newtown, Wigan. Although so badly wounded

The Finest of All

that he needed months of recuperation at home, Green was just thankful to be alive. He had survived the Gallipoli campaign and a stint in the Middle East where he was promoted to Commissary Sergeant. One day a group of about twenty dirty, smelly desert tribesmen, led by a British officer, arrived at his supply depot. "Give them what they want," ordered Green's Commanding Officer. Only much later did he realise that he had kitted out the famous Lawrence of Arabia.

At Guillemont even after months of artillery bombardment the barbed wire was still intact.. Attack after attack failed. An expert grenade thrower, Harry Holcroft, was loaned to another unit to soften up a German trench defending the village:-

"I lobbed six bombs and then the men went over the top."

The Officer then ordered Harry to go over as well but he declined saying:-

"I was only lent to throw bombs."

Nevertheless, Harry was made to go and was almost immediately wounded in both legs. Of the rest, only one man came back:-

"I got into a shell hole, there was somebody dead underneath and he was heaving with maggots and lice. Later on in the afternoon, something dropped on me. A Liverpool Jock. There was a sniper about and I said only move a bit."

The sniper kept them both pinned down so Harry thought up a plan to get rid of him:-

"I said, just put up your hand (sic) and pull it back. he did it. Ping! I said I've took t'pin out of't bomb, do it again.'

The Liverpool volunteer did so and the sniper was spotted behind a fallen tree. Harry threw his last two grenades and silenced him.

The fighting had become so severe that a new injury appeared, shell-shock. Sergeant Charles Baldwin, R.F.A., of Wigan recounts how he came across one such case:-

> "We got very heavily shelled for about half an hour. I found an infantryman lying in the road in front of the battery. I went to give him a hand and I found he had shell-shock very bad and it took me all my time to get him to move."
> W.E. 5th. August, 1916.

The German shelling recommenced and Baldwin bundled the man, paralysed with fear, into a small slit trench which already held seven men:-

> "The poor fellow got stuck in the entrance preventing me getting in. The Boche knocked me in and the next I remember was being dug out."
> W.E. 5th. Aug., 1916.

Another lucky soldier was Lance-Corporal John Mallin of the Border Regiment:-

> "We reached the trenches about daybreak and the Germans started to shell us when we arrived and kept it up all day not stopping for one minute. The old German trenches were battered in so we dug ourselves in as well as we could in the pouring rain. A shell burst buried three of us. We got out and another one burst against us. We got out and another one burst against us. I felt my hair stand on end and cannot relate proper how I did feel but when I tried to speak, I found I couldn't."
> W.E. 28th. September, 1916.

It was about a month before he recovered his powers of speech. Artillery now dominated the battlefield as both sides struggled for the Thiepval Plateau. Nowhere was safe:-

> "I will never forget my first visit to the front line in a hurry. As we were marching up the road to the trenches a shell dropped close by me killing the man marching at my side and wounding a

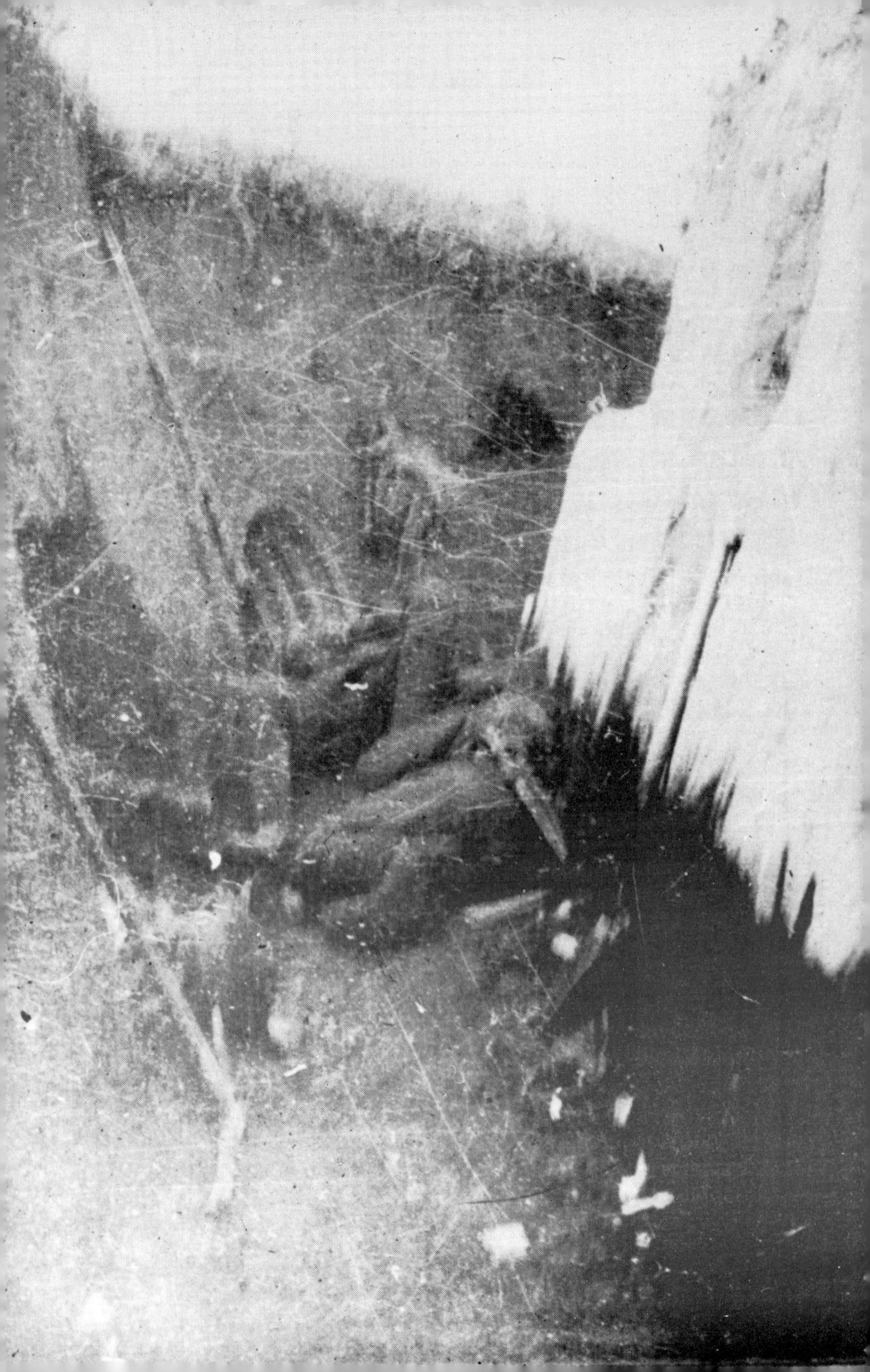

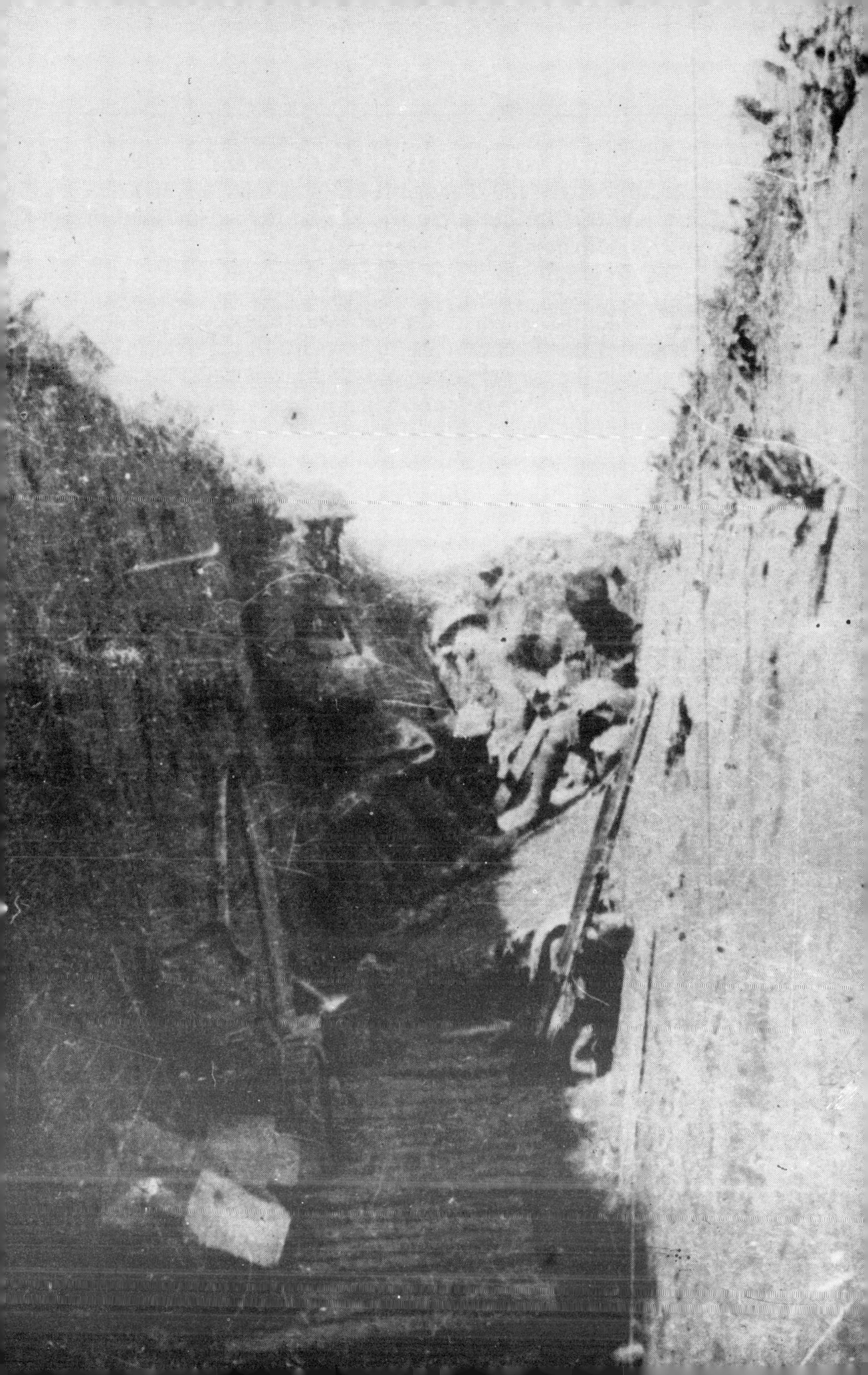

few more and as soon as we got in the trenches, one dropped a yard from me. All the damage it did was bury me and turn me from a white man into a nigger. My rifle was smashed in my hands by another shell.'
W.E. 19th. Sept., 1916

The front line dug-outs, where the men were supposed to shelter and rest when not on watch, were useless against artillery. Private Taylor, a Golborne man in the King's Own Royal Lancaster Regiment, was asleep in one with two companions when it received a direct hit by a shell killing all three. Aged only 31 years, he left a widow and four children. Corporal Moody a Wiganer in the Field Artillery, was only wounded when, with four comrades, he was resting in his dug-out when it too was hit by a shell.

On the attacking infantry exposed to the enemy's fire as they crossed No.-Man's-Land, the German artillery rained down death. Sergeant Fred Dale took a philosophical view:-

> "On several occasions I have had to go through his (German) barrage of shell fire, running across a place where troops have to cross to join an attack. You can either wait until it lifts or turn back which you never do or double through it and take your luck. When it is safely negotiated, you look back and scratch your head and simply marvel how you have done it."
> W.E. 9th. Sept., 1916.

Lance Corporal Sylvester of Wigan was one of those who got safely across this exposed section then:-

> "The order came to move on and we had just come out in Indian file when a shell burst just in front of me killing two of my pals instantly. I felt a shock and my shoulder belt and baggage 'vamoosed'. A minute later I felt something wet running down my leg. Of course it proved to be a red spurting fountain and then I became a surgeon with my own field dressing. I rested for an hour behind the trunk of a big tree which had been blown across the road until the R.A.M.C. arrived. All the time there was perfect hail of shells."
> W.E. 19th. Aug., 1916.

Naturally the Germans used artillery in support of their own counter attacks. Lance Corporal Walter Mercer of Woodfield Street, New Springs, was killed during such an attack. As German shells crashed down on his trench, he kept his machine-gun firing as long as he could. It was estimated by the survivors that he had killed about seventy Germans before a shell blew up his position.

On the 16th. September, 1916, the British tried again and impatiently used their new secret weapon, the tank, before large enough numbers of them had been built to make a significant impact. Following a three-day bombardment, eighteen tanks, supported XV Corps in a dawn attack. Although few in numbers, their effect was sensational, The Germans were amazed and terrified at the sight of these monsters. A Wiganer, who took part in the attack, wrote home:-

> "Headed by the 'tanks' which hypnotised the Germans, we went straight across No-Man's-Land and emptied belts of cartridges from our machine-gun into the panic-stricken Huns. We got a good many prisoners who seemed very frightened."
> W.E. 10th. Oct., 1916.

Before the war, Charles Bell had worked in his father's seed shop in Market Street, Wigan. He had been refused enlistment in the army during the Boer War because he was too young. A keen cyclist, he had enlisted in the Cycling Corps and had been transferred to tanks in time to take part in the very first attack. The armour plating had not been fixed properly and a ricocheting bullet came through a gap and hit him in the seat of his pants! The day's gains were the greatest since the battle began. Part of the original German third line was taken. But there were too few tanks. Another opportunity for a major strategic breakthrough was lost and once more the fighting degenerated into stalemate.

The Germans counter-attacked regularly and on the 25th. September, Corporal Peter Crompton of the Grenadier Guards, who before the war had been a collier at Long Lane Colliery, was one a half a dozen men holding a trench when it was overrun by Germans. Although two of his comrades were killed and the other three were wounded, Crompton remained unscathed, winning the Military Medal as a determined attack was beaten off. On the same day his nephew Private John Hasleden, who enlisted alongside him in the same regiment at the same time, was wounded in another attack. A month later in October, another Grenadier Guardsman, Sergeant Herbert Hall, of Richmond Street, Wigan, also won the Military Medal, for bringing in a wounded man to safety under heavy fire.

On 29th. October, 1916 George Walsh, of the Lancashire Fusiliers, a sapper attached to the Royal Engineers Tunnelling Company, was in a dug-out near Fricourt, when it was blown up by a German mine. The survivors were buried, unconscious and menaced by gas, while shells exploded all around them. For two hours, Walsh dug out the three men left alive, spent another two hours giving them artificial respiration then dragged them to safety, eight hours in all. For this courageous act, he received the D.C.M., only the Victoria Cross was a higher award. When he got back to Wigan, he was given an official reception in the Town Hall by the Mayor.

What kept the men going in such terrible conditions? Many reasons have been given, religion, patriotism, discipline, courage and loyalty, not just to their Country, their Army and their Regiment but to their comrades who were often their fellow townsmen. Motives varied. Colonel Darlington, who commanded the 1/5Manchesters, a territorial battalion raised entirely of men from the Wigan, Leigh and Atherton districts, wrote an admiring opinion of their qualities while on active service during the Gallipoli camapign a year earlier:-

> "They were blessed with an unquenchable sense of humour, an ability to stick to it, great self reliance and an apparently natural esprit de corps, the last two virtues being due, I imagine, to the nature of their work down the pit and that they were very loyal to their Trade Union."
> Darlington, 'Letters Fom Helles', P.12.

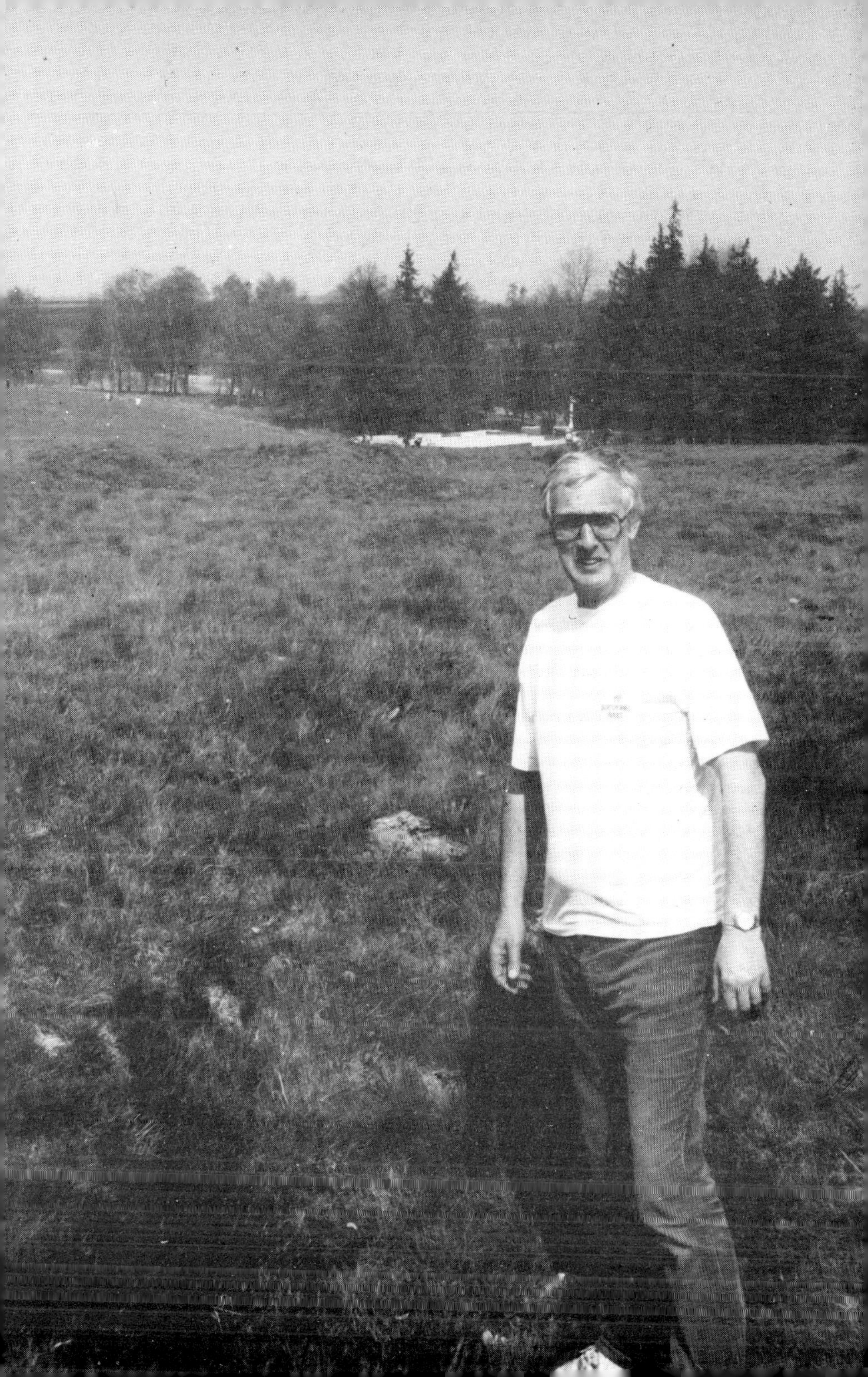

Private Walker had a philosophical outlook:-

> "When I was in the thickest of the fighting I often thought of my mother's words, 'it is as God wills it'".
> L.J. 14th. July, 1916.

There was no doubt that religion played a big part. Private McDonald recorded that on the 1st. July as he returned across No-Man's-Land:-

> "We passed many of our own dead. In one place we passed one poor chap lying dead in a small hole. He was lying on his side where, in his hand, he held an open Testament. I could not stop but I have always wondered what page he was reading."
> W.O. 29th. July, 1916.

Another reason was that in 1916, the ordinary British soldier still felt he was doing the right thing. Often, in his letters home, he turned his anger on the various types of men who were reluctant to volunteer, the shiftless, the cowards, the genuine pacifists. A Corporal in the Royal Engineers summed up the feelings of many in a letter home to his wife in Leigh:-

> "I have been surprised that so many of my pals have gone under and yet I am proud of the fact that I am a soldier and like the others I am prepared to face death. Just by here we have many conscientious objectors, the men who preach but do not fight. Religion comes as a useful cloak for the shirker. The heroic Christ who died to abolish sin is dishonoured by these men. Virtue is manliness and valour and resentment against cruelty and wrong. No coward or shirker can be a Christian if he refuses to help fight and crush the immoral and devilish Hun."
> L.J.7th. July, 1916.

Those who were of military age and fitness but not yet in the forces were despised by those fighting, especially the volunteers. A Wigan soldier, wounded and home on leave wrote to the local paper:-

> "After a few hours rest, I took a stroll round the good old town and found to my amazement a large number of strapping young men. Well, I could not say they were all men or they would not be there. After six months of graft in the trenches and short handed at that, I did not think I should find so many eligible young men left in the good old town."
> W.E. 1st. Jan., 1916.

He went on to describe how he had asked half a dozen why they were not in uniform and had received a variety of evasive replies.

> "What I ask is, do the people of Wigan know what the state of affairs is out in France and Flanders? Lads who are doing spells in the trenches of twelve and fourteen and sometimes seventeen days and nights in mud which, on average, is knee deep. I don't think they do. Does the slacker know that it is through him that this is necessary? Do they know the homes, the sweethearts, these lads have left for such as they? Let me, through your paper, appeal to these men to consider their position."
> W.E. 1st. Jan., 1916.

The men in the trenches saw very little difference between those who would not fight through indifference, laziness, hostility to the War or cowardice but made no attempts to justify their actions, lumped together as 'shirkers' and those who claimed to be 'conscientious objectors' to the principle of war. R.A.M.C. Private A.W. Hunt's views, ironically published in the local paper on the opening day of the Somme battle, are caustic:-

> "Some of the excuses I have seen put forward by so-called conscientious objectors are absurd, if not downright wicked. If they could hear comment passed on their excuses by the Tommies out here, I am sure that even their pathetic consciences would be pricked."
> W.E. 1st. July, 1916.

Most volunteers, without previous military experience wondered if and hoped that, they would be up to the task ahead. Sergeant J.J. Grace of the Royal Field Artillery, in civilian life, a Leigh postman, put down his feelings in a poem which was only to be sent home if he were killed in action:-

"I Will Be Worthy Of It

I may not reach the heights I seek
My untried strength may fail me.
Or, halfway up the mountain peak
Fierce tempests may assail me.
But though that place I never gain
Therein lies comfort from my pain beyond
And so for me there is no sting in death
And so the grave has lost its victory.
It is but a crossing with abated breath
And white set face a little strip of sea
To find the loved ones on the shore
More beautiful more precious than before.
And that is death."

He was killed on the 23rd. June, 1916 on the eve of the opening preliminary bombardment.

At dawn on the 13th. November, after several postponements for bad weather, one final attempt was made, this time at the northern end of the battlefield which had not seen action since the 1st. July, 1916. This time, helped by early morning mist and by the men moving tactically from cover to cover, most objectives were taken, even the seemingly impregnable Beaumont Hamel. After four days' fighting, 6.000 German prisoners were captured. As the first winter snows fell, both sides collapsed exhausted and could fight no more. The Battle of the Somme was over.

The Finest of All

MAP 8: GROUND GAINED:- 1ST JULY — 19TH NOVEMBER 1916.

———	British trenches 1 July.
◨◨◨	Gained 1 July.
— · — · —	" " 13 July.
— — —	" " 14 July.
– – – –	" " 12 September.
· · · · · ·	" " 18 September.
x — x — x —	" " 27 September.
x x x x x	" " 19 November.

0   1   2   3
Miles

- Gommecourt
- Serre
- Beaumont Hamel

GERMANS

- Thiepval
- Pozieres
- Flers
- High Wood
- Delville Wood
- Trones Wood
- Mametz Wood

BRITISH

- Albert
- Fricourt
- Mametz
- Montauban

FRENCH

CONCLUSIONS

Analysis of the Somme campaign has always been dominated by the horrific casualties, especially those on the first day, yet hindsight shows that the battles had profound consequences for the way the remainder of the war was conducted. For the first time since the war began, Britain had taken the major role in an offensive, their French allies were reassured of British commitment and what had hitherto been a rather shaky alliance, was steadied. The losses themselves had a lasting impact on the British public. After such sacrifices there could be no turning back. It would have been a betrayal of the dead. For the British Army, it removed any lingering doubts about the ability of the Kitchener volunteers. When James Fleming of Lord Street, Hindsford, formerly a miner at one of Fletcher Burrows' collieries and now a Sergeant in an East Lancashire battalion, was wounded by a rifle grenade, his officer wrote to reassure Fleming's wife that the wound was not serious, adding:-

> "It has been largely through N.C.O.s of your husband's type that the new armies have been such a success."
> L.J. 14th. July, 1916.

Just as importantly the German capacity to fight was severely weakened. The Somme, together with Verdun, took a heavy toll on their best professional officers, N.C.O.s and peace-time trained soldiers. Despite their own terrible losses, the rank and file British volunteers, realised how much they had achieved against the world's finest conscript army (even if their estimate of the consequences was over optimistic):-

> "Our Derby Army[1] are knocking off his best troops and now it is only a matter of time."
> W.O. 5th. Aug., 1916

Private McDonald from Ashton-in-Makerfield, a more thoughtful and perceptive writer expressed similar views:-

---

[1] The writer, Private Michael Nolan, was from one of the divisions recruited by Lord Derby.

> "We have been in close contact with the enemy and have found ourselves his equal and in some cases, his superior in nerve and resource."
> W.O. 29th. July, 1916.

From 1916 onwards, German recruits fought on the same footing as their British counterparts. No longer did they have years of training behind them and the morale of the ordinary German soldier does seem to have plummeted. A letter from Private Darby of Plank Lane, Leigh is typical of several which give similar imformation:-

> "One of our Company, the smallest kid we have, brought in twenty one Germans with only a revolver. When they surrender they shake hands with one another and laugh with glee once they get behind our lines. Then when our heavy artillery shelled their lines, they started laughing fit to burst."
> L.J. 3rd. Nov., 1916.

The German generals realised that they needed a stronger trench system and in 1917, they withdrew their divisions on the Somme front to a new specially and secretly prepared defensive network, the Hindenburg Line. This was indeed an impregnable position but when, in March, 1918, Germany launched one last desperate attack, in an attempt to win the war and actually broke through for fifty miles, the offensive failed to push the British Army into the sea. The Germans had started from too far back. If they had begun from their old Somme position, the advance would have reached its objective. In this respect, the Somme saved the war.

More importantly, after the Somme battles, the German military hierarchy realised that the war on land was unwinnable. Even Ludendorf conceded that *'the German Army has been fought to a standstill and is utterly worn out.'* He feared that Somme-type fighting would be inflicted on other parts of the Western Front and that, *'our troops would not be able to withstand such attacks indefinitely if the enemy give us no time to rest.'* At a conference in 1917, at which unrestricted submarine warfare was discussed, the German Army leadership supported their Naval colleagues' request for this widening of the war at sea. Thumping the table, Hindenberg gave as his reason,

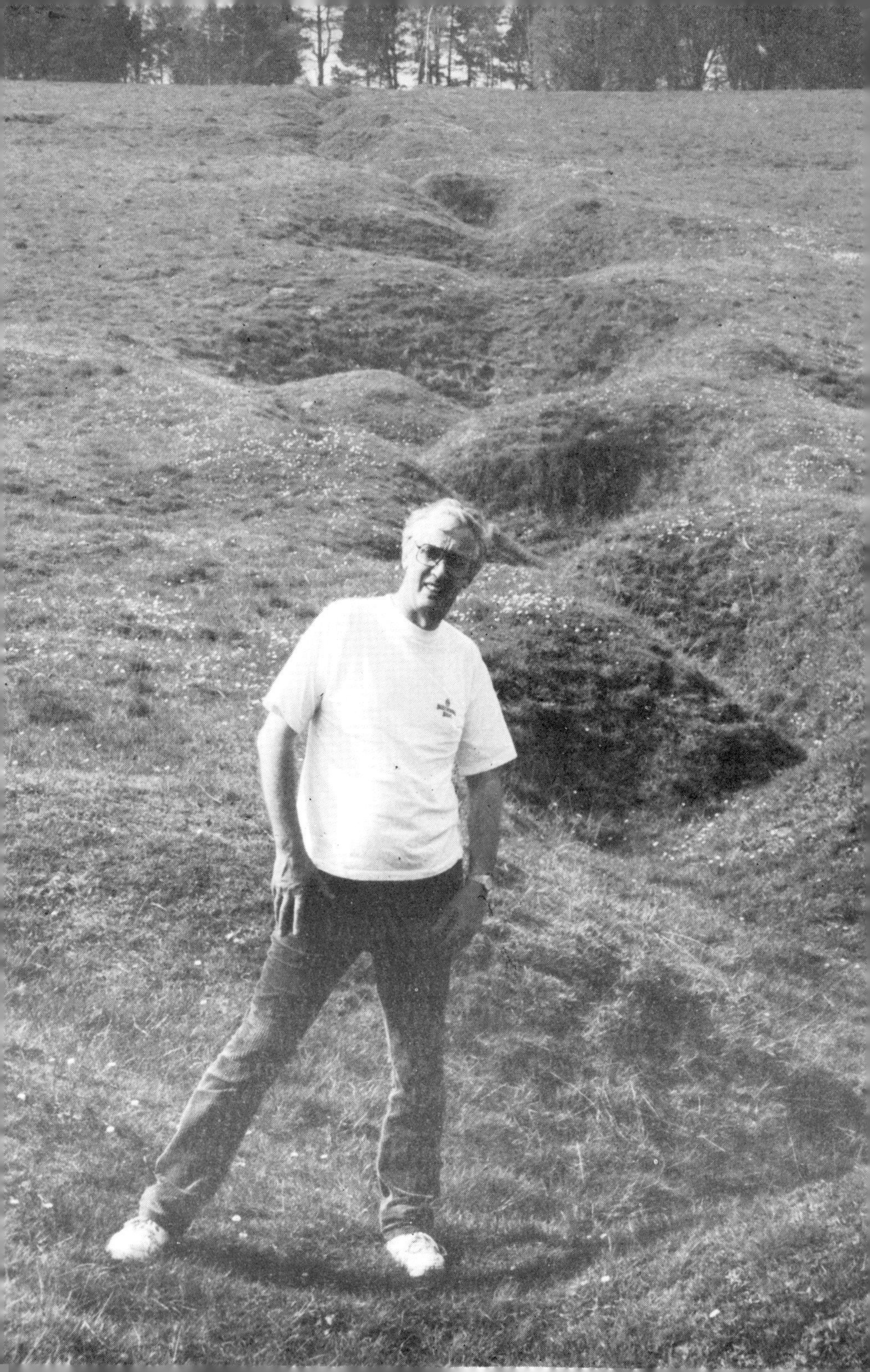

'the need to save the men from another Somme.' As a result of the indiscriminate sinking of merchant shipping, America entered the conflict on the side of the Allies and the war was lost for Germany.

The real tragedy of the Somme lies in the unlearned lessons of the battlefield. True, the British developed better co-operation between the infantry and the artillery so that in future attacks the infantry advanced behind a 'creeping barrage' sometimes as slowly as twenty five yards per minute. Tragically, British attacking formations remained unchanged, attacks continued to use the tactics of advances in successive waves of soldiers, ideal targets for unsubdued machine-gun fire. Lightly equipped fighting patrols should have led the attacks to break into the defences before the machine-guns could be brought out. It was ironic that on the 1st. July, 1916, the symmetrical lines torn apart by machine-gun and artillery fire broke formation into such groups but they were too few in number and lacked cohesion, co-ordination and leadership.

It was doubly unfortunate that, while the British persisted in their outmoded methods of attack, the Germans, who were for the most part on the defensive, recognised their system's deficiencies and reorganised their tactics. The ideas that no ground was to be abandoned and that lost ground must immediately be retaken at all costs, were both given up. Instead, a flexible defence in depth was devised with more emphasis on local counter attacks, and local commanders taking more initiative. Their new methods were soon to show good results during the offensives of the following months. The consequences of the Battle of the Somme were far reaching, although they were not those predicted by the British Army High Command. The agony of the British soldier was not over.

The Battle of the Somme helped to win the war but at what cost! Local men played their part in that victory and the locality paid its share of the price.

Lest We Forget.

THOSE WHO FELL, 1st. July, 1916.

Over one hundred men, either local or with local connections were killed in action on the 1st. July, 1916, the first day of the Battle of the Somme, a greater number than on any other single day of the First World War although 4th. June, 1915 and the 8th. to 9th. August, 1915 in the Dardanelles also saw heavy local losses[1]. Some men died on that day, (K.I.A. - killed in action), some died of their wounds (D.O.W. - died of wounds), during the days that followed, some were reported missing in action (M.I.A. - missing in action), and were only subsequently listed as killed. Those men who have been traced are listed below with as much personal information about them as it has been possible to collect. There may be others.

Lest we forget.

ANDERS Joseph, 18717 Lance Corporal, 11/Royal Inniskilling Fusiliers (Donegal and Fermanagh), 16, Warrington Road, Wigan, aged 38 years, collier at Worsley Mesnes Colliery, left a widow and five children. K.I.A., 1st July, 1916. No known grave.

ASPINALL George, 18217, Corporal, 1/Border Regiment, 22, Caroline Street, Higher Ince, aged 23 years, drawer at Moss Hall Colliery, Ince, left a widow. K.I.A, 1st. July, 1916. No known grave.

BAILEY George William, 29184 Private 1/Royal Welch Fusiliers, 24, Schofield Lane, Wigan, aged 24 years, collier for Cross Tetley & Co., left a widow and two children, had been in France one week. K.I.A. 1st. July, 1916.

BALL Henry, 7698 Private, 16/Manchester Regiment (1st. Manchester Pals), 14, Tunnicliffe's New Row, Plank Lane, Leigh, aged 21 years, single, enlisted September, 1914, Sunday School Teacher at Leigh United Methodist Church, platoon runner and best shot in the Company. M.I.A. 1st. July, 1916. No known grave.

BARLOW Robert, 16828 Private, 1/King's Own Royal Lancaster Regiment, 153, Poolstock, Wigan, aged 31 years, single, M.I.A. 1st. July, 1916. No known grave.

[1] See companion volume, 'Just Like Hell. Local Men in the Dardanelles.'

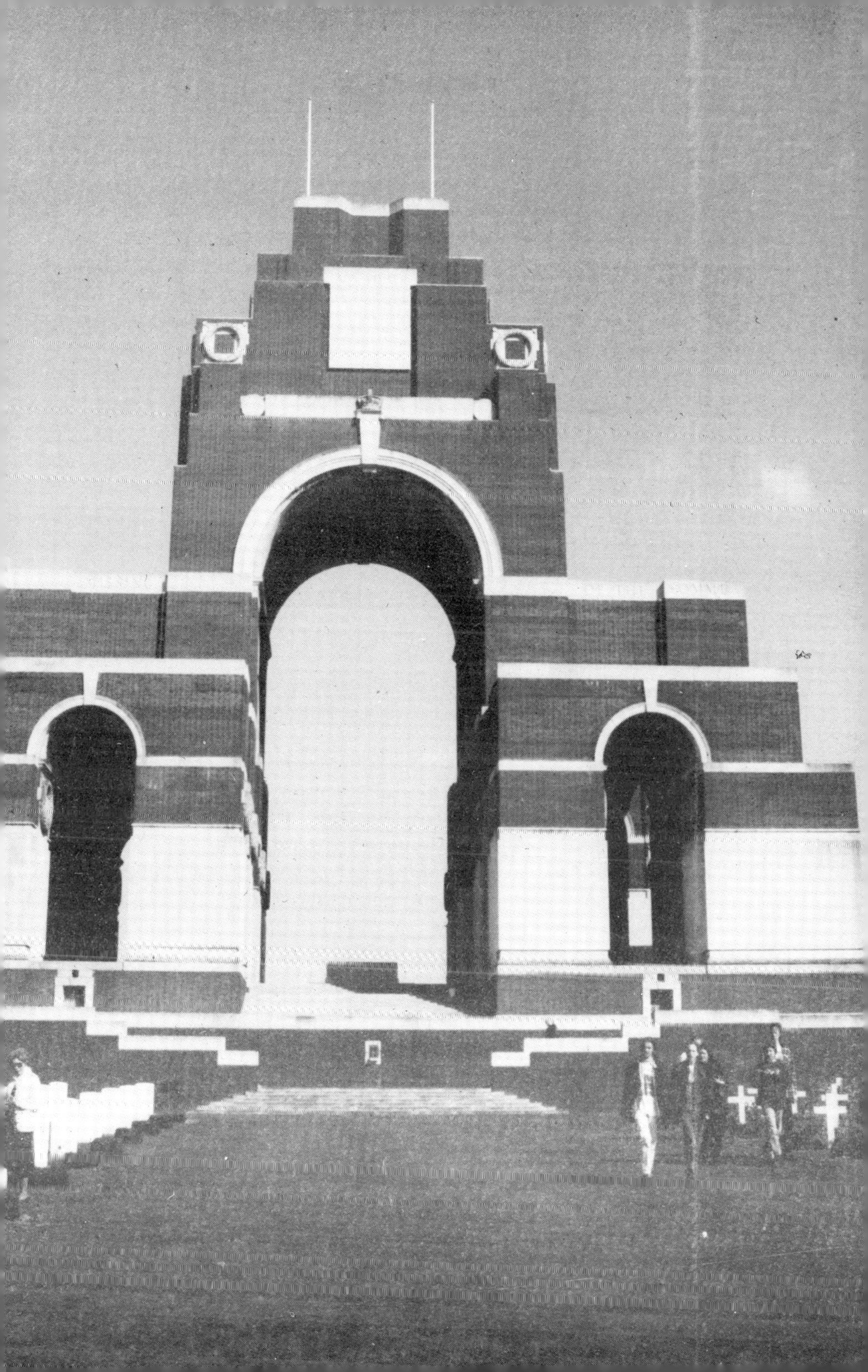

The Finest of All

BENTLEY Herbert, 19045 Private, 1/Border Regiment, 4, Victoria Street. Platt Bridge, left a widow and children. K.I.A. 1st. July, 1916. No known grave.

BRISCOE Fred, 29387 Private, 1/Lancashire Fusiliers, 6, Sefton Street, Leigh aged 21 years, single, hairdresser and window cleaner, his father was the trainer of Leigh Rugby Club. K.I.A. 1st. July, 1916.

BROOKS John, 27264 Private, 11/East Lancashire Regiment (Accrington Pals), 16, Grayson's Yard, Wigan. K.I.A. 1st. July, 1916. No known grave.

BRYAN Thomas, 18682 Private, 20/Manchester Regiment (5th. Manchester Pals), 3, Dingle Fold, Astley, collier at Nook Pit, awarded the Military Medal for carrying wounded to safety, left a widow and seven children. K.I.A. 1st. July, 1916.

BURNS Thomas, 18080 Private, 1/Lancashire Fusiliers, 36, Bridge Street, Hindley, aged 32 years, widower, K.I.A. 1st. July, 1916. No known grave.

BOYDELL James, 18888, Private, 1/Border Regiment, Hindley, K.I.A. 1st. July, 1916. No known grave.

CHADWICK Fred, 18352 Private, 20/Manchester Regiment (5th. Manchester Pals), 36, Battersby Street. Leigh aged 36 years, single, manager of Leigh Co-operative Society's butcher's shop at Bag Lane, Atherton. K.I.A. 1st. July, 1916.

CLEGG Thomas, 15300 Private, 9/York and Lancaster Regiment (Pontefract), 6, Talbot Street, Lank Lane, Leigh, aged 32 years, collier, left a wife and three children. K.I.A. 1st. July, 1916. No known grave.

CUNLIFFE Fred, 33592 Private, 22/Manchester Regiment (7th.Manchester Pals), born in Hindley but living in Chicopee, near Springfield. Massachusetts, U.S.A. when war broke out and returned to enlist, his nearest relatives lived at 298, Whelley, Wigan. K.I:A. 1st. July, 1916. No known grave.

DAVENPORT James, 3935 Private, 1/Lancashire Fusiliers, 204, Parr Bridge, Mosley Common, Astley. K.I.A. 1st. July, 1916.

DAVIES Edward, 25587 Private, 1/Royal Welch Fusiliers, 18, Jury Street, Westleigh, collier at Westleigh Colliery, left a widow and seven children. K.I.A. 1st. July, 1916.

DICKINSON Alfred, 95 Private, 2/Lancashire Fusiliers, 8, Bolton Street, Wigan aged 32 years, posted missing in action, his body was found twelve months later buried in a shell hole. K.I.A. 1st. July, 1916.

DICKINSON William, 18895 Driver, Royal Field Artillery attached to 179 Brigade, 8. Bolton Street, Wigan, brother of Alfred above, killed on the same day, 1st. July, 1916 but not on the Somme.
DUMMICAN Hugh, 10934 Private, 15/Lancashire Fusiliers (1st. Salford Pals), 56, Talbot Street, Leigh, aged 27 years, single, collier at Bickershaw Colliery. K.I.A, 1st. July, 1916.
EDGE Richard, 14012 Private, 1/King's Own Royal Lancaster Regiment, 28, Chester Street, Leigh, aged 32 years, single, brewery worker, wounded in the Dardanelles. K.I.A, 1st. July, 1916. No known grave.
EDWARDS John, 17167 Private, 1/King's Own Royal Lancaster Regiment, 24, Holt Street, Westleigh, single, collier for the Fletcher Burrows' Coal Company, his death meant that his widowed mother had now lost both her sons as his elder brother had been killed at Loos early in 1915. D.O.W. 3rd. July, 1916.
ENTWISTLE Harry, 33056 Private, 22/Manchester Regiment (7th. Manchester Pals), Humphrey Street, Higher Ince, single, aged 19 years, booking clerk Lancashire and Yorkshire Railway. His father was the School Attendance Officer for Ince. K.I.A. 1st. July, 1916.
FAIRCLOUGH John, 18489 Private, 2/Border Regiment, Heath Charnock near Standish. K.I.A. 1st. July, 1916. No known grave.
FAIRHURST William Joseph, 19128 Private, 1/Lancashire Fusiliers, Leigh, aged 24 years, collier at Westleigh Colliery, had survived frostbite in the Dardenelles, left a widow. K.I.A. 1st. July, 1916.
FARLEY Charles, 9064 Corporal, 1/Border Regiment, 13, Miry Lane, Wigan, single, after serving ten years in the army, came home from India at the outbreak of war, had survived the Dardanelles campaign. M.I.A. 1st. July, 1916.
FARRINGTON Walter, 14671 Private, 1/Lancashire Fusiliers, Worthington, near Standish, D.O.W. 7th. July, 1916.
FEREDAY Joseph, 16010 Private, 8/York and Lancaster Regiment (Pontefract), 19, Nelson Street, Tyldesley. K.I.A. 1st. July, 1916.
FINN Michael, 188897 Private, 1/Border Regiment, born County Mayo, Ireland, living and enlisted in Wigan, had survived the Dardanelles campaign, left a widow. M.I.A. 1st. July, 1916. No known grave.
FINNEY William 17889 Private, 11/East Lancashire Regiment (Accrington Pals), 10, Park Road, Orrell, aged 21 years, single, porter at Orrell railway station. M.I.A. 1st. July, 1916. No known grave.

The Finest of All

FOSTER James, 16045 Private, 12/ Manchester Regiment, 6, Wright Street, Whelley, Wigan, late of 3, Heaton Street, Standish, aged 22 years, collier at Victoria Pit, Standish, left a widow and one child. D.O.W. 8th. July, 1916.
FOSTER John, 18107 Private, 1/Lancashire Fusiliers, Green Bank Street, Tyldesley, aged 33 years, collier at Astley & Tyldesley Coal Company, left a widow and seven children all aged under ten. D.O.W. 20th. July, 1916.
FRIAR Samuel, 25664, Private, 22/Manchester Regiment (7th. Manchester Pals), aged 22 years, born in St. Helens, living at 20, Jury Street, Leigh, collier at Sovereign Pit, Westleigh, last seen carrying a wounded officer across No-Man's-Land through an artillery barrage. K.I.A. 1st. July, 1916. No known grave.
GENT Joseph, 16893 Private, 1/King's Own Royal Lancaster Regiment, born in Ince, had been working in Chorley, left a widow and five children. K.I.A. 1st. July, 1916.
GERRARD James Henry, 15812 Private, 8/York and Lancaster Regiment (Pontefract), 11, Green Street, Atherton, aged 25 years, single, collier at Chanters Colliery, Atherton. K.I.A. 1st. July, 1916. No known grave.
GOODWIN George, 1912 Private, 1/Lancashire Fusiliers, 181, Glebe Street, Leigh, aged 27 years, single, foundry worker, had been wounded twice in the Dardanelles. K.I.A. 1st. July, 1916.
GORDON Mark, 1039 Private, 2/Lancashire Fusiliers, 34, Holland Street, Wigan, aged 26 years, single, played rugby for Swinley Hornets. D.O.W. 3rd. July, 1916. No known grave.
GREGORY Charles, 955 Sergeant, 8/York and Lancaster Regiment, 263, Bolton Road, Aspull, aged 22 years, single, collier at Scot Lane Colliery, Blackrod. M.I.A. 1st. July, 1916. No known grave.
GRUNDY Arthur, 20108 Private 15/Royal Scots Fusiliers (Edinburgh Pals), Bryn Hall, Bamfurlong, aged 22 years, single, clerk at Worsley Menses Ironworks, secretary of Bamfurlong Primitive Methodist Sunday School. K.I.A. 1st. July, 1916. No known grave.
GRUNDY James Franklin, 29463 Private, 2/Lancashire Fusiliers, 101, Chapel Street, Bedford, Leigh, aged 26 years, tailor at Boydell and Sons, Market Street, Leigh, Superintendent of Leigh Unitarian Sunday School. K.I.A. 1st. July, 1916.
HIGGINSON William, 1589 Lance Corporal, 12/Manchester Regiment, 3. Henrietta Street, Leigh, aged 21 years, single, compositor

at Leigh Chronicle, teacher at Leigh Wesleyan Sunday School. K.I.A. 1st. July, 1916. No known grave.
HOLDEN Joseph, 24209 Private, 11/ East Lancashire Regiment (Accrington Pals), born Leigh. living in Blackburn, aged 23 years, single, pawnbroker. K.I.A. 1st. July, 1916. No known grave.
HUDSON Charles, 12274 Private, 1/Lancashire Fusiliers, 3, Boardman Street, Leigh, aged 25 years, collier at Astley Colliery, veteran of the Dardenelles. M.I.A. 1st. July, 1916. No known grave.
IRONS Thomas, Private, York and Lancaster Regiment, 61, Belle Green Lane, Higher Ince, aged 32 years, collier at Wombwell Colliery near Barnsley, left a widow and two children. K.I.A. 1st. July, 1916.
JACKSON Albert, 14629 Private, 6/Loyal North Lancashire Regiment, 20, Neville Street, Ince, aged 18 years, single, left a widowed mother and several brothers and sisters. K.I.A. 1st. July, 1916.
JACKSON, Alfred, 13103 Private, 1/King's Own Scottish Borderers. D.O.W. at home, in Tyldesley, 19th. July, 1916.
JACKSON George, 17404 Private, 15/Royal Scots Fusiliers (Edinburgh Pals), 25, Bedford Square, Leigh, aged 28 years, left a widow and one child. K.I.A. 1st. July, 1916. No known grave.
JOHNSON Charles Joseph, 16385 Private, 7/South Lancashire Regiment, 69, Plank Lane, Leigh, aged 25 years, drawer at Bradshaw Colliery, killed by a sniper while carrying water up to the front, left a widow and two children. K.I.A. 1st. July, 1916. No known grave.
JONES Richard, 11012 Private, 15/ Lancashire Fusiliers (1st. Salford Pals), Wigan. K.I.A. 1st. July, 1916.
JONES William, 25867 Private, 7/Yorkshire Regiment (The Green Howards), 8, Pilling Street, Leigh aged 18 years, single, piecer at Alder Mill. K.I.A. 1st. July, 1916.
KEMP Thomas, 2nd. Lieutenant, 20/Manchester Regiment (5th. Manchester Pals), 'Gorse Bank', St. Helens Road, Leigh, aged 27 years, single, chartered accountant, rugby union player for Leigh, Manchester and Lancashire. K.I.A. 1st. July, 1916.
KNOWLES Albert Edward, Private, 2/Gordon Highlanders, 8, Scot Lane, Blackrod, left a widow. D.O.W. 7th. July, 1916.
LANGTON John Thomas, 12000 Private, 1/Border Regiment, 18, Farrimond's Yard, aged 30 years, collier for Pearson and Knowles Coal Company, had survived the Dardenelles campaign and the

sinking of the troopship *'Royal Edward'*[1], left a widow and one child. K.I.A. 1st. July, 1916. No known grave.

LANCASTER John, 25508, Private, 22/Manchester Regiment (7th. Manchester Pals), Wigan. K.I.A. 1st. July, 1916.

LARNEY Thomas, Private, 2/Royal Scots Fusiliers, attached to 139 Machine Gun Company, aged 27 years, cafe owner in Railway Road, Leigh, left a widow. K.I.A. 1st. July, 1916. No known grave.

LINDSAY Francis Howard, Captain (temporary Major), 1/14County of London Regiment (London Scottish), aged 40 years, administrator in the Scottish Education Department, fourth and second surviving son of Mr. W.A. Lindsay, K.C., grandson of the late Mr. Colin Lindsay, therefore a relative of the Earl of Crawford, educated at Malvern and Cambridge, left a widow and two children. K.I.A. 1st. July, 1916. No known grave.

LIVESLEY John William, 19211 Private, 1/Lancashire Fusiliers, 18, Victoria Street, Higher Ince, aged 18 years, single, collier at Maypole Colliery. M.I.A. 1st. July, 1916.

LOMAX James, 25780 Lance Corporal, 18/King's Liverpool Regiment (2/Liverpool Pals), aged 27 years, Wardour Street, Atherton, clerk at Atherton Co-op. K.I.A. 1st. July, 1916. No known grave.

LOWE Joseph, 19132 Private, 1/Border Regiment, 6, Bolton Street, Higher Ince, aged 24 years, collier at Abram Colliery, left a widow and one child. K.I.A. 1st. July, 1916.

LOWE Thomas, 19219, Private, 15/Durham Light Infantry, 27, Kendrick Street, Wigan, collier at Wardley, County Durham where he enlisted with his work mates, left a widow and three children. K.I.A. 1st. July, 1916. No known grave.

LOWTON Alfred, 20064 Private, 1/Essex Regiment, formerly in the Royal Horse Artillery, Standish, member of the local brass band. D.O.W. 1st. July, 1916.

MAJOR Samuel, 18986 Private, 1/Border Regiment, 10, Lower St. Stephen Street, Wigan, aged 18 years, single, member of All Saints Church Lads Brigade, had enlisted in 1914 aged 16. M.I.A. 1st. July, 1916.

---

[1]His description of the sinking is contained in the companion volume, 'Just Like Hell'.

MESSER James Henry, 1506 Private, 22/Northumberland Fusiliers (3rd.Tyneside Scottish), born in Manchester Road, Ince, aged 30 years, collier in Sunderland where he enlisted with his workmates, left a widow and four children. D.O.W. 4th. July, 1916.

MORGAN William James, 11996 Corporal, 2/South Wales Borderers, 6, Arderne Street, Wigan, left a widow and two children. K.I.A. 1st. July, 1916.

MORRIS James, 17826 Private, 1/East Yorkshire Regiment, 17, Banner Street, Hindley, left a widow and three children. K.I.A. 1st. July, 1916. No known grave.

MULRANEY Patrick, 11885 Private, 1/Border Regiment, 47, Lorne Street, Wigan, aged 22 years, single, a drawer at Low Green Colliery. One of three brothers killed during the war, Edward Mulraney (Royal Engineers) 12th. August, 1918 and William Mulraney (Machine Gun Corps) 14th. October, 1918 were killed in France shortly before the Armistice. M.I.A. 1st. July, 1916.

MEYERS Tom, 18991 Corporal, 2/Border Regiment, 46, Walmer Street, Poolstock, Wigan aged 21 years, collier for Crompton and Shawcross Limited, left a widow and two children. K.I.A. 1st. June, 1916. No known grave.

McGRAIL John, 28700 Corporal, 9/Cheshire Regiment, attached to King's Liverpool Regiment, 18, Worsley Street, Golborne, aged 33 years, single, collier at Golborne Colliery, one of six brothers in the Army. K.I.A. 1st. July, 1916. No known grave.

McCABE Peter, 3518 Private, 1/Lancashire Fusiliers, 26, Silver Street, Wigan aged 46 years, had served in India, Sudan and South Africa, left a widow and one child. D.O.W. 7th. July, 1916.

ORMESHER Herbert, 13363 Lance Corporal, 1/Lancashitre Fusiliers, 77, Beech Hill Lane, Wigan. K.I.A. 1st. July, 1916. No known grave.

OWENS Richard, 9314 Private, 12/ Manchester Regiment, born in Wigan but living in Oporto, Portugal when war broke out and returned to Atherton to enlist. K.I.A. 1st. July, 1916. No known grave.

PARKER Richard, 17735 Lance Corporal, 10York and Lancaster Regiment, Beech Hill, Wigan. D.O.W. 3rd. July, 1916. No known grave.

PEAK Norman, 2nd. Lieutenant, 12/Manchester Regiment, aged 24 years, single, Cambridge University graduate, old boy of King William's School, Isle of Man, only son of the owner of James Peak &

Co., tarpaulin manufacturers of Wallgate, Wigan. K.I.A. 1st. July, 1916.

PEAK James Chadwick, 52546 Private, 9/Cheshire Regiment, Wigan. K.I.A. 1st. July, 1916. No known grave.

PENDLEBURY Thomas, 9358 Private, 17/Manchester Regiment (2nd. Manchester Pals), 122, Higher Green, Astley, aged 46 years, colliery at Astley Colliery, left a widow and five children. K.I.A. 1st. July, 1916. No known grave.

PENNINGTON Thomas, 19288, Private 2/Border Regiment, Pemberton, Wigan. D.O.W. 7th. July, 1916.

PHILLIPS William, 7421 Private, 16/ Manchester Regiment (1st. Manchester Pals), aged 21 years, single, Austin's Farm, Lostock. K.I.A. 1st. July, 1916. No known grave.

PICKUP Herbert, 8297 Sergeant, 1/East Lancashire Regiment, a postman in Haigh, left a widow who lodged in the Gibraltar Inn, Scholes. K.I.A. 1st. July, 1916. No known grave.

PILKINGTON John, 42199 Private, 1/Lancashire Fusiliers, 36, Melbourne Street, Wigan, aged 22 years, single, collier at Pearson and Knowles Colliery. K.I.A. 1st. July, 1916. No known grave.

PEARSON William, 17544 Private, 1/King's Own Royal Lancaster Regiment, 1, Off Lime Street, Wigan, collier at Kernishaw Nook Pit, Leigh, left a widow and two children. M.I.A. 1st. July, 1916. No known grave.

POUNCEY William, 18744 Private, 11/ Royal Inniskilling Fusiliers (Donegal and Fermanagh), 2, Anderton Street, Wigan, left a widow and two children. K.I.A. 1st. July, 1916.

RICHARDSON William, 13669 Bombardier, 171/Brigade Royal Field Artillery, 192, Poolstock Lane, Wigan, aged 23 years, single, collier at Long Lane Colliery. K.I.A. 1st. July, 1916. No known grave.

ROSCOE Robert, 20188 Private, 1/East Lancashire Regiment, aged 28 years, 4, Earl Street, Belle Green Lane, Ince, left a widow. K.I.A. 1st. July, 1916. No known grave.

ROUGHLEY William, 25065 Private, 15/Lancashire Fusiliers (1st. Salford Pals), Ormskirk. K.I.A. 1st. July, 1916.

ROWLANDS Joseph, 16042 Corporal, 8/York and Lancaster Regiment, Coal Pit Lane, West Leigh, aged 23 years. D.O.W. at home, 11th. July, 1916 from wounds received on 1st. July, 1916 and is buried in Leigh Cemetery, Plot 34, Row L, Grave 9. Why not visit?

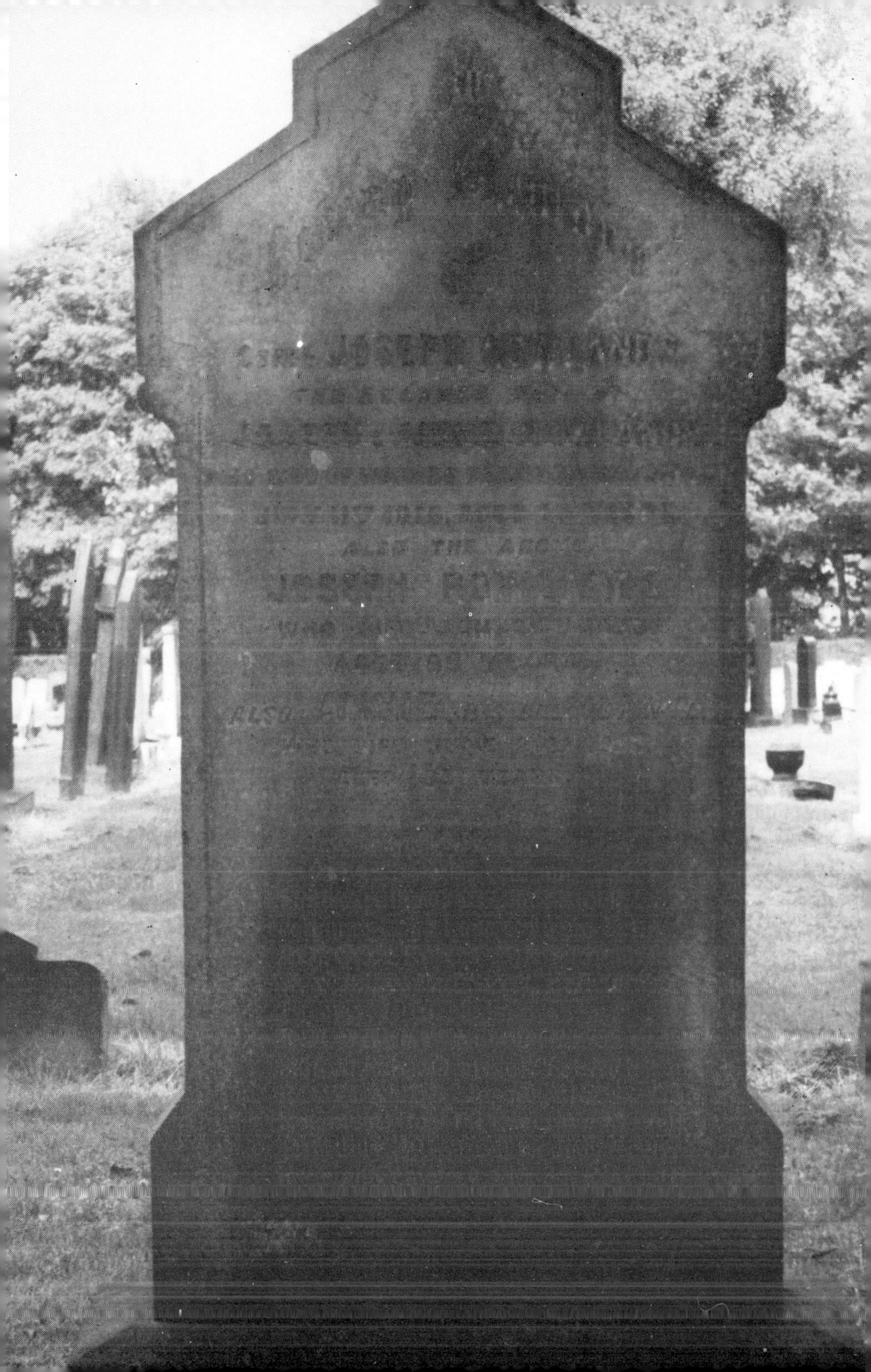

RUDD John Allan, 18120 Private, 10/Loyal North Lancashire Regiment, a signaller attached to the Machine Gun Corps, 245, Firs Lane, Leigh, aged 22 years, single. D.O.W. 9th. July, 1916.
REYNOLDS William, 16043 Private, 8/York and Lancaster Regiment (Pontefract), Tyldesley, born Hindsford. K.I.A. 1st. July, 1916.
SIXSMITH Richard, 22935 Private, 20/King's Liverpool Regiment (4th. Liverpool Pals), Upholland. K.I.A. 1st. July, 1916. No known grave.
SMALLSHAW Robert, 17216 Private, 1/Kings Own Royal Lancaster Regiment, Atherton. K.I.A. 1st. July, 1916. No known grave.
SMITH Thomas, Private, R.A.M.C. (attached to the Gordon Highlanders), 270, Firs Lane, Leigh, aged 40 years, dataller at Abram Colliery, well known local singer. D.O.W. 2nd. July, 1916.
SOUTHERN Harry, 16667 Lance Corporal, 8/York and Lancaster Regiment (Pontefract), 17, Manchester Road, Tyldesley, aged 25 years, spinner at Caleb Wright's cotton mill, left a widow and five children. K.I.A. 1st. July, 1916. No known grave.
STATHAM Robert, 29385 Private, 1/Lancashire Fusiliers, 74, Siddow Common, Leigh, aged 20 years, single, worked at Messrs. Shaw and Co's brewery. K.I.A. 1st. July, 1916. No known grave.
STOTT Edward, 1021 Private, 14/York and Lancaster Regiment, Wigan. K.I.A. 1st. July, 1916. No known grave.
SUTTON Jack, Sapper, Royal Engineers, Alfred Street, Tyldesley, aged 27 years, single, 0ccupation unknown, played Northern Union for Leigh Shamrocks and Leeds. K.I.A. 1st. July, 1916.
TENNIEL George Arthur, 17771 Lance Corporal, 20/Manchester Regiment (5th. Manchester Pals), Tyldesley. D.O.W. 2nd. July, 1916.
TAYLOR James Illes, 20763 Private, 2/Kings' Own Yorkshire Light Infantry, 6, Sougher's Lane, Bryn, Ashton-in-Makerfield, left a widow and two children. K.I.A. 1st. July, 1916.
THICKNESSE John, Lieutenant Colonel, 1/Somerset Light Infantry, aged 46 years, son of Bishop Thicknesse, former Rector of Wigan and grandson of Ralph Thicknesse former Mayor of Wigan, left a widow and three children. K.I.A. 1st. July, 1916.
TOMLINSON Josiah, 20443, Private, 2/Border Regiment, 90, Bridge Street, Golborne, aged 43 years, collier at Golborne Colliery. D.O.W. 23rd. July, 1916.

TONGE Herbert, 17030 Private, 1/King's Own Royal Lancaster Regiment, 484, Tyldesley Road, Tyldesley, single, cotton spinner. K.I.A. 1st. July, 1916. No known grave.

TOPPING Robert, Private, 1/Border Regiment, Talbot Road, Leigh, aged 21 years, single, half-back for Leigh Rugby Club. K.I.A. 1st. July, 1916.

TROWBRIDGE Henry, 5445 Private, 1/Lancashire Fusiliers, Wigan. K.I.A. 1st. July, 1916.

TUCKER Arthur, 1330 Lance Sergeant, 2/Lancashire Fusiliers, Wagon and Horses, Millgate, Wigan, aged 25 years, born in Rochdale, left a widow and had survived dysentery, jaundice and enteric fever in the Dardanelles. M.I.A. 1st. July, 1916.

WARD Joseph, 21046 Private, 11/East Lancashire Regiment (Accrington Pals), 19, Ashton Street, Wigan, aged 25 years, collier at Abram Colliery, left a widow and two children. K.I.A. 1st. July, 1916. No known grave.

WARING William, 19150 Private, 1/Border Regiment, Hindley. M.I.A. 1st. July, 1916. No known grave.

WIELDING James Henry, 9503 Private, 17/Manchester Regiment (2nd. Manchester Pals), 59, Manchester Road, Astley. K.I.A. 1st. July, 1916.

WHITE John. 18931 Private, 1/Border Regiment, Higher Ince, collier Hindley Green Colliery, left a widow. M.I.A. 1st. July, 1916. No known grave.

WILCOCK Fred, 7289 Lance Corporal, 1/East Lancashire Regiment, Chorley. K.I.A. 1st. July, 1916.

WILLIAMS Sydney Robert, 11384 Corporal, Royal Engineers, Leigh. D.O.W. 1st. July, 1916.

WILLIAMS Fred, 153741, Sapper, Royal Engineers, Ashton-in-Makerfield. D.O.W. 3rd. July, 1916.

WINSTANLEY John, 19151 Private, 1/Border Regiment, 136 Lily Lane, Platt Bridge, aged 21 years, single, collier. K.I.A. 1st. July, 1916. No known grave.

WOOD William, 20853 Private, 1/King's Own Royal Lancaster Regiment, Warrington Road, Newtown, Wigan, aged 31 years, collier Pemberton Colliery, left a widow and one child. D.O.W. 3rd. July, 1916.

The Finest of All

YATES Arthur Hilton, 11492 Private, R.A.M.C. attached to the King's Royal Rifle Regiment, 77. Barnsley Street, Wigan, aged 21 years, single. hit by a shell and killed instantly. K.I.A. 1st. July, 1916.
YOUNG John William, Private, R.A.M.C. attached to 2/Gordon Highlanders, aged 24 years, single, collier at Golborne Colliery. K.I.A. 1st. July, 1916.

Entries marked 'No Known Grave' are inscribed on the Thiepval Memorial, (see photograph), over one hundred and forty feet high and the largest British war memorial in the world, carrying the names of over 73,000 men who fell on the Somme sector of the Western Front and who have no known grave. The exact position of each entry can be obtained from the six-volume alphabetical Memorial Register found in most local libraries, or direct from the Commonwealth War Graves Commission.

Other entries are of men buried in marked and numbered graves in the dozen or so Commonwealth War Graves cemeteries in the Somme sector and their exact final resting place can be obtained from the cemetery registers found in most local libraries, or direct from the Commonwealth War Graves Commission.

Commonwealth War Graves Commission, (formerly the Imperial War Graves Commission) 2, Marlow Road, Maidenhead, SL6 7DL. Tel:- (01628) 34224.

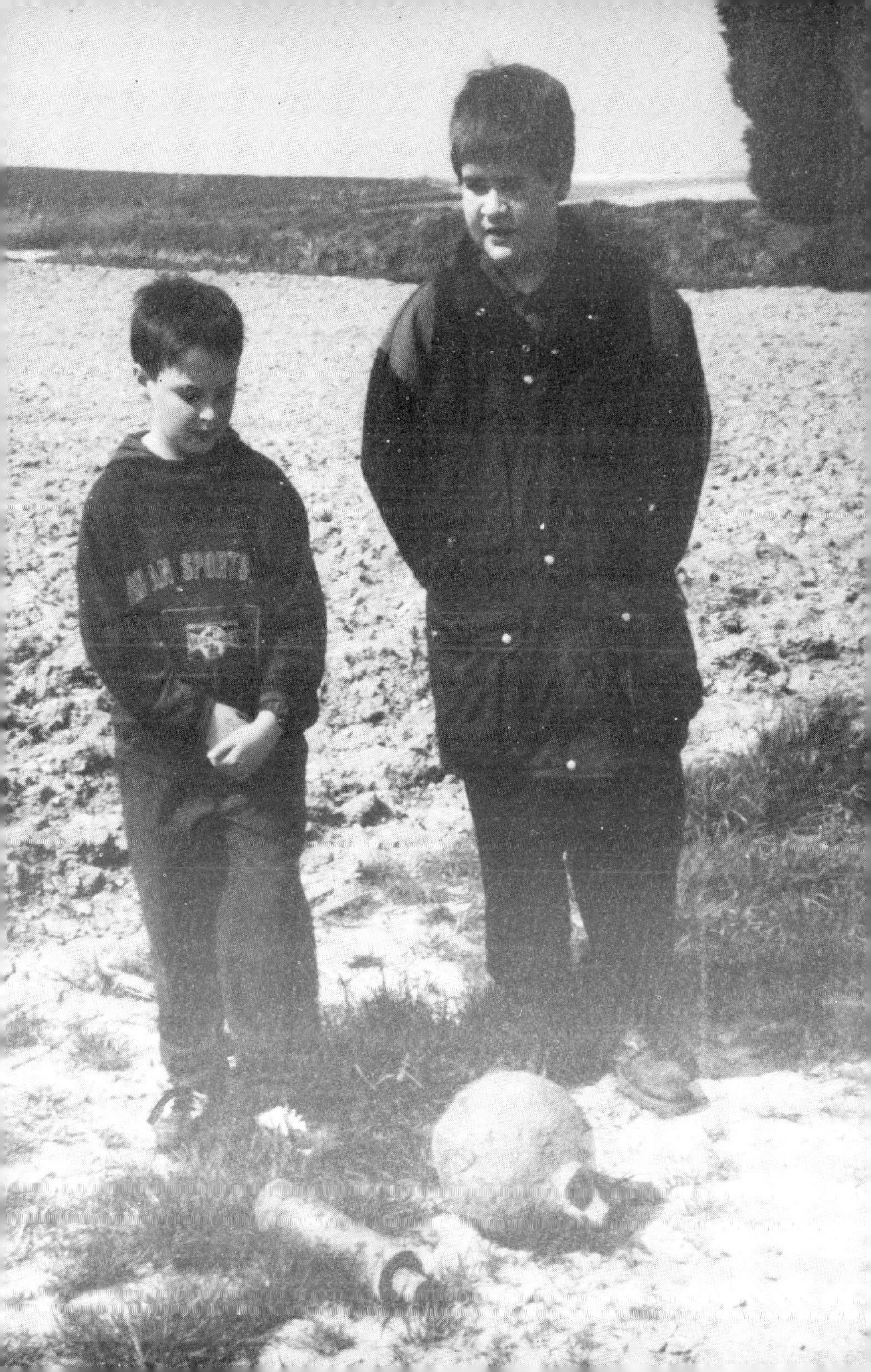

IN EPITAPH

One year later, on the nearest weekend to the first Anniversary of the opening day of the Battle of the Somme, remembrances of some of the fallen appeared in the 'In Memoriam' columns of the 'Wigan Observer' and the 'Leigh Journal'.

ANDERS.
In loving, memory of my dear husband, Lance Corporal Joseph Anders, killed in action, 1st. July, 1916.

> None knows how sad the parting
> Or what the farewell cost,
> But God and his Holy angels
> Have gained what I have lost.

Sadly missed by his wife and children 16, Warrington Road, Wigan

BRISCOE.
In loving memory of Fred Briscoe, killed in action, 1st July, 1916, aged 23 years.

> Days of sadness still come o'er us
> Tears in silence often flow.
> Ever well our hearts remember
> The dead son we lost a year ago.
> When day dawns and shadows flee
> Thy purpose Lord we then shall see.

From his sorrowing father, mother, sisters, brothers and sister-in-law. Leigh.

CHADWICK
In loving memory of private Fred Chadwick who was killed in action 1st. July, 1916

> He heeded his nation's bidding
> He answered his country's call.
> He gave his life for his country
> And the welfare of us all.
> Too far away thy grave to see
> But not too far to think of thee.

From his loving brother and sister. Leigh.

EDGE
In loving memory of Private Richard Edge, killed in action, 1st. July, 1916.

> There on the field of battle
> He calmly took his place.
> He fought and died for Britain
> And the honour of his race.

From his loving brother. Patricroft, Manchester.

JACKSON
In Loving memory of Private Harold Jackson who fell in action, 1st. July, 1916.

> He gave himself willingly when his country called.

From his mother, sisters and brother. 20, Melville Street, Ince.

KNOWLES
In loving memory of Private Albert Edward Knowles, Gordon Highlanders, who fell in action, 1st. July, 1916.

> He sleeps besides his comrades
> In a hallowed grave unknown
> But his name is written in letters of love
> In the hearts he left at home.
>
> May the heavenly winds blow softly
> O'er that sweet and hallowed spot.
> Through the sea divides his grave from us
> He never will be forgot.

Sadly missed by his wife, father, mother, sisters and brothers. 8, Scot Lane, Blackrod.

LARNEY
In loving memory of Private T. Larney, Royal Scot's Regiment (sic) killed in action, 1st. July, 1916.

> Tom. God gave you to me as a blessing
> And you have taught me to know
> That those whom God have joined
> Together, Death cannot put asunder.

Ever remembered by your wife, Polly. Manchester.

> We think of him in silence
> And his voice we oft recall
> But there's nothing back in answer
> Save his photo on the wall.

From sorrowing mother and sisters, Leigh.

MAJOR
In loving and affectionate reminiscences of our dear son and brother, Private Samuel Major, Border Regiment, killed in action, 1st. July, 1916 in his eighteenth year.

> Gone is the face we loved so dear
> Gone is the voice we longed to hear
> Far away from sight and speech
> But not too far from thoughts to reach
> There come a mist in the blinding rain
> And life will never be the same

From his father, mother, sisters and brothers. 10, Lower St. Stephen Street, Wigan.

MORRIS
In loving memory of my dear husband, James Morris, 1st. East Lancashire Regiment, killed in action, 1st. July, 1916.

> The silent grief that's in my soul
> No human eye can trace
> For many an aching heart lies hid
> Behind a smiling face.
> We cannot Lord thy purpose see
> But all is well that's done by thee.

Ever remembered by his loving wife Edie and his children, Mildred, Ethel and Thomas. 17, Banner Street, Hindley.

PICKUP
In fondest memory my dear husband Sergeant H. (Bert) Pickup, reported missing, 1st July, 1916 and presumed killed on that date.

> Only those who have loved and lost
> Known the meaning of the word gone.

From his sorrowing wife, Ada.

STATHAM
In loving memory of my dearly beloved son Robert Statham, killed in action, 1st. July, 1916.

Somewhere in France the shadows softly fall upon a silent grave
Where our loved one has been sleeping with England's fallen brave.
To that unknown grave far away
A mother's thoughts wander today.
Unknown to the world he stands by my side
And whispers, 'Do not fret, death cannot divide.'

Always remembered by his mother, father, sisters and brothers. 74, Siddow Common, Leigh.

TAYLOR
In loving memory of my dear husband, Private James Illes Taylor, King's Own Yorkshire Light Infantry, killed in action, 1st. July, 1916.

Afar he sleeps, the cannon's roar
Disturb his calm repose no more.
What though no voice of home was near
To soothe with love his dying ear
The cloud has passed from that dear brow
It glows in Heaven's clear brightness now.

Rest calmly, rest for thou thy part has played
On this world's stage and death thy hand has stayed.
Thy work is done, thou'st laid thy armour down
Fought the good fight and gained the eternal crown.

From his loving wife and children. Sougher's Lane, Bryn. Ashton-in-Makerfield.

TONGE
In loving memory of Private Herbert Tonge, killed in action, 1st. July, 1916.

> Sleep on dear brother in your unknown grave
> Your life for your country you nobly gave.
> No-one stood near to say goodbye
> But in God's keeping safe you lie.

Ever remembered by his loving sisters. 90, Mealhouse Lane, Atherton.

WINSTANLEY.
In loving memory of Private John Winstanley. Border Regiment, killed in France, 1st. July, 1916.

> If we could have raised his dying head
> Or heard his last farewell
> The grief would not have been so hard
> For these who loved him well.
>
> We think of him in silence
> And his name we oft recall
> But there is nothing left to answer
> But his photo on the wall.

From his loving father, mother, brother, sisters. 136, Lily Lane, Platt Bridge.

HALLIWELL

HE ANSWERED HIS COUNTRY'S CALL
SACRIFICING ALL
FROM FATHER, MOTHER
BROTHER AND SISTERS

PHOTOGRAPHS

Frontispiece — Probably one of the most poignant photographs taken during the First World War.

Page 9 — Such was the rush of volunteers that there were not enough weapons. In any case it was dangerous to let some of them near a loaded rifle.

Page 13 — An extremely rare photograph of the extended order formation being practised.

Page 19 — A German machine-gun with a full crew. One was found with the gunner chained to it.

Page 23 — Once the fighting was over both sides mingled and helped one another towards the casualty treatment stations.

Page 29 — On the eve of the attack, the First Battalion of the Lancashire Fusiliers are addressed by their divisional commander, Major General H. de B de Lisle. A few days later, three-quarters of them were casualties, 164 killed, 308 wounded and 11 missing from the total of 697 officers and men who went over the top.

Page 35 — The German surface defences were pounded to bits but their deep dugouts saved the men inside from annihilation.

Page 39 — A rare photograph of the survivors from the Manchester Regiment returning from Montauban.

Page 40 — Some idea of the cover afforded by the sunken road half way across No-Man's-Land is shown by this photograph taken in 1995.

Page 56 — The village of Beaumont Hamel rebuilt from the ruins with No.-Man's Land now cultivated farmland. Taken 1995.

Page 60	The Hawthorne Mine crater is now filled with thick vegetation, mainly brambles and quite inaccessible, the interior impossible to photograph. Taken in 1995.
Page 69	This photograph of Montauban Allée trench must have been taken only minutes after its capture.
Page 70	The captured German trenches had to be quickly converted to British use in case of an immediate counter-attack.
Page 75	Ploughing has smoothed over the cratered battlefront but a few shell holes remain in the Newfoundland Memorial Park where as much as possible of the battlefield is preserved. Taken in 1995.
Page 76	The former deep trenches have been weathered to their present shape but their exact position can still be seen in this photograph taken in 1995.
Page 85	The magnificent Thiepval Memorial dominates the Somme landscape. No photograph can do it justice.
Page 93	This is a poor quality photograph but the actual headstone in Leigh Cemetery, Plot 34, Row L, Grave 9, is a moving tribute. Why not visit?
Page 99	Even today, eighty years later, French farmers are ploughing up battlefield debris, usually barbed wire but occasionally something more lethal. The object on the left is a British trench mortar shell while the German one on the right is definitely unexploded.
Page 100	Just one of the thousands of headstones which mark the last resting places of British soldiers in the Commonwealth War Graves cemeteries across France, beautifully kept and cared for by their devoted gardeners.